CREATING YOUR DREAM KITCHEN

HOW TO PLAN AND STYLE THE PERFECT SPACE

CREATING YOUR DREAM KITCHEN

HOW TO PLAN AND STYLE THE PERFECT SPACE

SUSAN BREEN

STERLING PUBLISHING CO., INC.
NEW YORK

Opposite page
Sleek design elements and reflective
surfaces create chic urban style.

Previous page
An L-shape island improves the
function of this kitchen by integrating
a sink, microwave, and dining nook.

Created by Lynn Bryan, The BookMaker, London
Design by Rachel Gibson
Case Study Photography by Claude Lapeyre

Library of Congress Cataloging-in-Publication Data Available

Published by Sterling Publishing Co., Inc.
387 Park Avenue South
New York, NY 10016

© 2005 Susan Breen

Distributed in Canada by Sterling Publishing
C/o Canadian Manda Group, 165 Dufferin Street
Toronto, Ontario, Canada M6K 3H6

Distributed in Great Britain by
Chrysalis Books Group PLC
The Chrysalis Building, Bramley Road
London W10 6SP, England

Distributed in Australia by
Capricorn Link (Australia) Pty. Ltd.
P.O. Box 704, Windsor, NSW 2756, Australia

Printed in China
All rights reserved

Sterling ISBN 1-4027-1960-4

For information about custom editions, special sales,
premium and corporate purchases, please contact Sterling
Special Sales Department
at 800-805-5489 or specialsales@sterlingpub.com.

CONTENTS

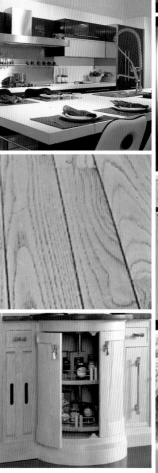

Part Two: Case Studies 90

Individual kitchens revealing the
answer to 10 different space
and lifestyle concerns.

WORKING WITH THE
PROFESSIONALS 156

Left   A centrally-located dining
table forms the social hub of a large
kitchen with an open floor plan.

INTRODUCTION

Designing and building a beautiful new kitchen is a dream come true; a once-in-a-lifetime opportunity to carefully craft the most important room in the home. A few decades ago, the typical residential kitchen was best characterized as a boxy, utilitarian space solely centered on food preparation. Walls isolated the cook from the social areas of the home; guests sat several rooms away passing time until the meal was served. Sometimes, guests wandered into the kitchen to chat, and when they did, found that socializing together in a less-formal setting was far more enjoyable than being sequestered in separate rooms. Thankfully, it did not take long before the kitchen replaced formal living and dining spaces as the new social hub of the home.

Architects and designers responded by reconfiguring the central living space of the home. Many interior walls have now vanished, the formal living room is gone, and the small, enclosed spaces have given way to large, airy, "gathering" rooms where cooking, dining, entertaining, and other activities now take place. What's more, updating older houses to reflect the shift has turned home remodeling into one of our fastest- growing industries. The fact is, the new kitchen is the pulsating heart of today's busy household.

When creating a new kitchen, freshening up the floor plan is just the start. Think of the new space as a rich canvas to create a personalized kitchen fitted with materials and features that reflect your style and support the way you cook, dine, relax, and entertain.

Great kitchens do not just happen; they are the result of meticulous planning and a careful evaluation of the space, as well as the people, who will use it.

The late, great Julia Child once shared a bit of her kitchen design wisdom with me. "Design your kitchen right the first time, and you will never have to think about it again." To organize some fifty

assorted sauté pans that Julia used on a regular basis, her husband devised a pegboard system. On it he traced an outline for each piece of cookware, ensuring that all had a permanent "home" in the kitchen. Likewise, when the couple noted that guests naturally congregated close to where Julia cooked, a comfortable seating area was added to the kitchen decades before anyone dreamed of entertaining in the kitchen. Her legendary kitchen was so carefully considered that she barely

Opposite page
Mid-Twentieth century elements mixed with modern materials produce a sleek-looking kitchen.

changed a detail over the forty years she cooked in it.

This book is devoted to bringing your vision of the perfect kitchen to life. Set aside the notion that great kitchens are reserved for those fortunate few with large spaces and unlimited budgets. Thanks to an ever-widening array of products and services available to the residential market, great design has never been more accessible. Today, regardless of the size of your project, or the scope of your budget, a dream kitchen is within nearly everyone's reach.

Throughout the book, you will find practical information to begin planning your kitchen, and beautiful photos to spark your imagination. The first half of the book is devoted to the basics of kitchen function and design. Here, you will discover that a thorough evaluation of your current kitchen might be best place to begin planning your new space.

You will learn about layout, how to set a budget, and the importance of establishing priorities to guide the decision making process.

Move ahead to the next section to familiarize yourself with the fundamentals of kitchen materials. Learn about the different types of cabinets and how the style you select is the most important design element to convey the tone of your new kitchen. Determine your storage needs and select the features that support your cooking and entertaining style. Evaluate surface options to strike a balance between form and function in your new kitchen. You will also learn that correct lighting is the key to creating a pleasing, adaptable space suited to a variety of tasks and activities.

In the second half of the book, you are invited to tour ten

magnificent kitchens chosen from around the country to reflect a range of architectural styles. Though each kitchen is wonderfully unique, all share inspired design and smart solutions that reflect the specific needs and desires of the household. As you view each space, note how the definition of 'dream kitchen' dramatically differs from one project to the next. For one home owner, a dream that began with the desire for a new cooktop evolved into a remodeled kitchen filled with family-friendly features. For

*Opposite page
Dark wood, painted cabinets, and polished marble surfaces give this city kitchen its sophisticated character.*

another, designing a kitchen in a seaside home fulfilled a lifelong dream of welcoming friends for leisurely weekends. Another dreamed of an adaptable city kitchen large enough for extended family, but cozy enough for a newly married couple. As you will see, these great kitchens are more than the sum of their parts. Though they begin with fabulous floor plans, gleaming appliances, and stunning stone surfaces, the dream is enjoying these spaces with family and friends.

Now it is your turn. On the following pages, you will learn how to plan, design and build a truly personalized new kitchen suited to the way that you live, for enjoying with the people who mean the most in your life. Have fun with the process. Take notes, start a file, visit showrooms, clip photos from magazines. And remember, all truly great kitchens begin quite simply...with a dream.

PART ONE

FUNCTION AND DESIGN

Sensational kitchens do not happen by accident. Rather, they are the culmination of an assessment of the needs of the entire household, and good planning. When it comes to great design, there is no such thing as 'one-size-fits-all.' The goal is to craft a kitchen based upon how people will use it, now and in the future. For most, it also means staying within a budget.

Setting a budget is dependant upon many factors. How much would you like, and are able, to spend? If you are remodeling, consider the age of the home and how long you plan to stay in it. Though remodels generally yield a high return on investment, if you spend too much, you may not recover the costs. Spending too little may not provide the appeal needed to attract buyers. A general guideline is to allocate between five and 15 percent of the home's current value for the kitchen; perhaps even as much as 20 percent if you are considering a custom space.

Remember that setting a budget is easy, sticking to it is another thing. Once you have finalized the amount, set aside ten to 20 percent as a contingency fund for changes because unforeseen costs are a reality.

Now carry out a thorough evaluation of your current kitchen. Jot down the activities that take place in the space during a typical day. For example, is more than one person involved in meal preparation and cleaning up? If so, you might benefit from two work triangles, or a second sink and dishwasher. If you have a family, do you dine together, or are meals staggered? The answer to that question could lead you to substitute a second oven with a warming drawer.

Look hard at task areas such as work surfaces, and storage. Make a list of kitchen systems that function well for you in your current space, and duplicate them in your new design. If you usually store spices and cutlery next to the range, and like that setup, repeat it. Also make note of ineffective systems that could be improved. For example, if the kitchen is crowded with people when you cook, select a layout that separates the cooking zone from the social areas.

List five favorite features of the current kitchen. Like the faucet with the built-in spray attachment and the pull-out storage system in the pantry? Then, list the five features that fall short of your expectations. Do you long for more counter space next to the sink? Need better light? Are you tired of having to search for cookware at the back of a dark base cabinet? Having completed both lists, use them when selecting new items.

Do you have space for a laundry, homework, internet browsing, television viewing, and bill paying in your current kitchen? If not, how could you configure the new space to include them?

In addition to the way the space is used right now, think about any changes you anticipate over the next five to 10 years. Will you be starting a family in the near future, or are you sending your youngest child off to college? Do you anticipate an elderly parent or person with physical limitations using the kitchen at some point? If the latter is possible, adding certain design features will make the area function more easily for a full range of mobility when that time comes.

Remember, this part of the process is about gathering information. No detail is too small, no dream too big. Take notes, talk to family members and consider every option. The more thought that goes into planning, the closer you come to creating an efficient, functional space in step with your lifestyle.

Left Glass-fronted cabinets act as a divider between the food preparation area and the informal dining/living space. A table at the end of the dividing unit can also be used as a food preparation area when necessary.

THE KITCHEN LAYOUT

A carefully considered layout is crucial to make the most of the available space available for your new kitchen and to provide the proper function of a variety of household tasks.

Planning a new kitchen from the floor up at the initial building stage gives you an opportunity to design a space tailored to your cooking style and personal design preferences. On the other hand, renovating an existing space might mean working within a structural framework of load-bearing walls, utility hookups, and existing doors and windows. However, with the latter, you can still push these boundaries with the decisions you make on style issues.

Regardless of the size and shape of your kitchen, meticulous planning to determine the proper layout is the key to transforming even the tiniest space into a

model of modern efficiency. Traditional kitchen design is loosely based upon a decades-old design principle known as the "work triangle." This concept relates to the movement of foot traffic between the sink, the range, and the refrigerator which are the primary task areas involved in food preparation. In theory, the perimeter of the triangle represents the least number of steps between the three points, thus creating a cooking and preparation zone as the cornerstone of an efficient kitchen layout.

Though the work triangle remains a useful planning tool when developing a layout, designers have expanded this concept

Below This New England-style large U-shaped kitchen features multi-level work surfaces, open shelving, and an island unit with several small drawers for utensils, linens, and chef's condiments. A movable unit has a marble top ideal for rolling pastry.

to include the household's style of cooking, as well as the complete range of activities that now take place in the space. When the concept was introduced 50 years ago, kitchens were designed around the way in which one cook prepared and cooked food in the area on his or her own. In today's multi-function, multi-faceted kitchens where cooking, entertaining, dining, and a host of other daily tasks take place, flexibility of use is the key to determining an efficient layout that lets you seamlessly shift from one activity to the next over the course of a busy day.

For that reason, contemporary kitchens may include two work triangles in households with more than one cook, or a modified triangle arranged around a second sink that may serve as a beverage center or a clean-up area for use during and after a meal.

Above A sleek single-wall layout organizes cooking, storage, and cleaning up tasks in a city-size kitchen. Upper cabinets open upward, and therefore require less space than traditional side-hinged cabinets.

UNIVERSAL DESIGN

▶ WHEN YOU PLAN YOUR KITCHEN PROPERLY THE FIRST TIME YOU CAN LOOK FORWARD TO IT PROVIDING YOU WITH A LIFETIME OF SERVICE. ONE WAY TO ACCOMPLISH THIS IS BY CREATING A KITCHEN THAT EASILY ADJUSTS TO ACCOMMODATE VARYING DEGREES OF MOBILITY. THE GOAL IS TO PROVIDE EASE OF USE FOR ANYONE WHO MIGHT BE USING THE KITCHEN, FROM YOUNG CHILDREN OR AGING PARENTS, TO AN OVERZEALOUS WEEKEND WARRIOR RECOVERING FROM A SPORTS INJURY.

FOR EXAMPLE, LOWERING A SMALL SECTION OF COUNTERTOP FROM THE STANDARD 36" (1M) HEIGHT DOWN TO 30" (75CM) HEIGHT CREATES AN ACCESSIBLE WORKSPACE THAT ALLOWS A SEATED PERSON, OR A CHILD, TO TAKE A PART IN PREPARATION OF A MEAL.

ANOTHER EXAMPLE: SIMPLY RAISING THE DISHWASHER 6" (15CM) FROM THE FLOOR ELIMINATES THE NEED TO BEND FOR LOADING OR EMPTYING THE APPLIANCE.

ALSO, IF YOU DECIDE ON A BANK OF OVENS, ENSURE THEY ARE PLACED HIGH ENOUGH SO YOU DON'T HAVE TO BEND DOWN TO TAKE HEAVY DISHES IN AND OUT OF THEM.

THE TYPES OF FAUCETS (FOR EASY MANIPULATION) AND THE CHOICE OF NONSLIP FLOORING AND GENERAL ACCESS ARE OTHER ISSUES TO CONSIDER.

TO LEARN MORE, ASK AN ARCHITECT OR A KITCHEN DESIGNER ABOUT THE BENEFITS OF UNIVERSAL DESIGN.

COMMON KITCHEN LAYOUTS

When it comes to kitchen layouts, bigger isn't necessarily better. Though the open and airy kitchens found in contemporary floor plans are perfectly suited to gathering and socializing, wide passageways and open spaces between task areas can pose problems for the cook.

To determine the most efficient layout for your kitchen, it pays to consult a design professional to thoroughly evaluate the available space and offer a choice of efficient layout options and design solutions. Though the size and configuration of your kitchen will determine the most beneficial layout, most layouts are based upon variations of the following basic design categories:

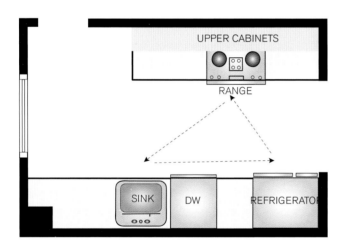

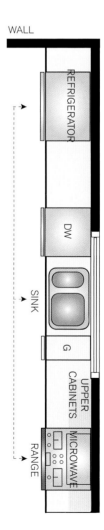

GALLEY

This is a compact design open at both ends with task areas lining both walls that enable the cook to easily move back and forth between the workspaces. On the downside, foot traffic that flows through the area may provide a distraction.

SINGLE WALL

In this layout, appliances and cabinets are arranged along a straight wall making it an ideal solution for a small kitchen. While this layout requires the cook to repeat steps, efficiency can be improved with the addition of a portable island workstation.

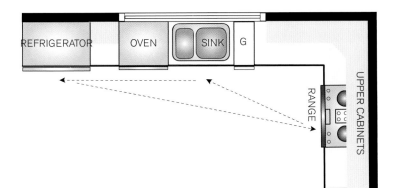

L-SHAPE

A layout characterized by a long stretch of cabinets adjacent to a shorter run, the L-Shape creates an elongated work triangle requiring extra steps between task areas. Any inconvenience is offset by the extra counter space.

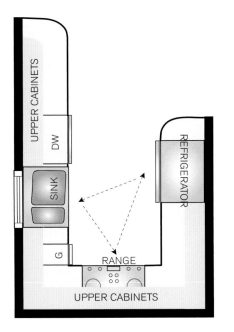

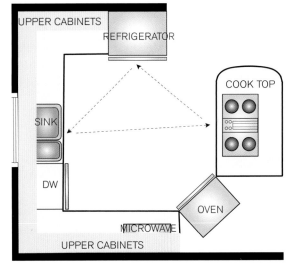

U-SHAPE

An efficient layout made up of three contiguous walls, provided the "U" is large enough to offer ample workspace. This design may be difficult for two cooks to function within unless modified to include a second work triangle.

G-SHAPE

This is a relatively new design that builds on the U-shape by attaching a peninsula at one end to create an extra workspace. While the enclosure shields the cook from foot traffic in the rest of the area, it can also make the kitchen feel smaller.

MEASURING YOUR KITCHEN

Accurate room measurements are essential for developing a budget and a design scheme for a new kitchen. If the plan calls for new construction, architectural drawings or blueprints will provide the information necessary to begin pricing features such as cabinets, countertops, and flooring. If you are remodeling without changing the floor plan, measuring before you visit showrooms is a time-saving step.

If you are remodeling but plan to alter the floor plan, some home design centers will create preliminary drawings useful for planning. Although most centers charge a small fee for this service, many will refund or deduct the sum if you place an order. Precise measurements are important to obtain accurate quotes, and are crucial if you plan to use them to place orders for cabinets or materials. Some manufacturers will insist on sending a representative to your home to finalize room measurements before accepting the order; those that do not will ask you to assume responsibility in the event that the cabinets do not fit the space.

Double-check all the dimensions, or ask someone to repeat the process to verify your results. Even minor errors can be costly.

To measure your kitchen, begin with the walls. Measure each wall from corner to corner and record the results in inches, rather than feet. For accuracy, measure the wall in three places: at floor level, halfway up the wall, and at the ceiling. Record the smallest

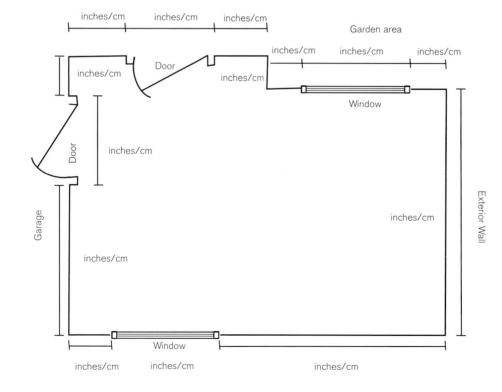

Left Here is a sample of a simple floor plan.
Draw up a plan like this, showing the items that are fixed, for example, plumbing, and any heating accessories such as a radiator. Add the exact measurements in inches/cm, not feet and yards/meters. Sizes for manufactured items are always given in inches/centimeters.

number but make note of variations for future reference. Use wall measurements to sketch a rough layout of the room on graph paper. Next, move in a clockwise direction around the room to measure the height and width of door openings and windows, including trim. Sketch those into the drawing. If wall openings include doors, indicate whether they swing into or out of the room. Include windows in walls by measuring the distance from the floor to the bottom of the trim, and from the top of the trim to the ceiling. Number the doors and windows as you move around the room. You can also draw separate sketches for each wall.

Then, evaluate individual walls to chart the room's fixed features. Include the placement of outlets, light switches, heating or air-conditioning vents, moldings, trim, built-in cabinets, closets, or any feature of the room that will part of the new kitchen.

Finally, measure the ceiling height from three different spots to account for any irregularities. For vaulted ceilings, measure the distance from the floor to the lowest point of the ceiling, as well as to the highest point of the ceiling. Include placement of skylights, soffits, and ceiling light fixtures.

When finished, add up the dimensions of each wall to see if they equal the overall measurements listed on the initial sketch. Add photographs of the room taken from a few angles. Include unusual features that may require special thought: an alcove, a small dining nook or a multi-level ceiling.

When the data is complete, organize drawings, measurements, and photos in a binder for future meetings with contractors and designers, or visits to showrooms.

The unfitted kitchen, which originated in 18th-century homes, is characterized by an assortment of armoires, dressers and sideboards that function as the primary work area.

The modern interpretation of this concept liberates the kitchen space from standard wall-to-wall cabinetry and countertops and redefines the area as a social space.

One of the major benefits is that the pieces can be moved about the kitchen, and can relocate when you sell up and relocate.

Free-standing cabinet interiors can also be fitted with storage system and topped with counters to create ample workspace.

If you are not ready to go completely unfitted, you can convey the charm of the unfitted style by using a blend of built-in and unfitted. Manufacturers have responded to this trend with units that create an unfitted look. For example, use conventional cabinetry in the cooking zone, but nearby you could add an antique dresser in which to store table linens and precious china, and a central island unit fitted with drawers and cabinets.

DINING STYLE IN KITCHENS

The role of the kitchen dining area has grown tremendously. Once little more than a small breakfast table and utilitarian chairs (with cushion pads for comfort if you were lucky) placed around it, this area has become the focus of social interaction.

Special occasion events that were once held in a separate dining room have moved into the larger, open-plan kitchen domain. Larger areas provide the opportunity to include a dining table and proper dining chairs. Meals are still eaten at a breakfast bar; however, that eating space, too, has become more sophisticated.

The challenge in creating a comfortable place for friends and family is to balance the dining area's visual connection to the rest of the room, with a sense of intimacy that establishes a warm, relaxing ambiance for dining. This is especially important in large kitchens where high ceilings and an open floor plan can leave the dining area floating in the middle of the room.

Consider the placement of the dining table and chairs at the early stage of the design phase. Ideally, the area should have natural light, and be sheltered from, yet connected to, the rest of the room. Ideally,

Left
A gracefully curved banquette in Art Deco style provides a comfortable seating area with sight lines to the cooking area. The fabric has been stain-proofed for easy care.

guests seated at the dining table should be able to carry on a conversation with the cook. A sense of shelter can be accomplished architecturally by slightly lowering the ceiling over the table, by building a half-wall that surrounds the dining area, or by designing an elevated dining platform one step up from the rest of the room. Often, something as simple as a change of flooring, lighting, or the color of a wall can alter the feel of one section of the kitchen without closing it off from the rest of the space.

If you are planning a remodel, consider a bump-out to create a dining alcove by enclosing a small porch or patio. You can achieve the same feeling by adding a built-in booth or curved banquette to an end or a corner of the kitchen.

Equally important is finding a table design that suits the scale of the dining area. A large table can dominate a space; one that is too small leaves no elbow room for guests. As a general guideline, allow enough room between the table and the wall for a person to comfortably pass behind a seated guest. To determine how many people a particular table will seat, count on a minimum of 25" (62cm) per place setting.

Buy the dining table that suits the way you entertain. In other words, if there are only four people in your household, choosing a table that seats eight to 12 (remember that antique pine refectory table you saw in a local antique shop?) could be a waste of precious space. Instead, consider a smaller table that opens up to accommodate extra place settings for when you hold special dinner parties.

Select the surface of kitchen dining tables and the material for chairs with comfort, durability, and ease of care in mind. Hard-wearing wood, stone, or laminate table tops are a better choice for constant daily use. Chairs should offer both comfort and back support. If cushions or seat pads are chosen, be sure that the covers are removable for cleaning, or choose treated fabric that repels soil and spills.

Above A demi-lune table is supported by a single stainless steel column that maximizes the available legroom for comfortable dining.

THE ISLAND KITCHEN

Few design concepts have had more impact on the modern kitchen than the addition of a center island. The island has become such an integral part of the day to day routine in many households that it is frequently used to anchor the central workspace and social areas of the kitchen.

If the kitchen is the heart of the home, then the hardworking island is the multi-functional hub of the central living space. Evolved from simple farm tables used to add extra workspace to small country kitchens, today's islands have become well-designed command posts, with features that keep the household running smoothly.

More interestingly, the island has altered the way we entertain. In large, open kitchens without walls, the island subtly separates food preparation and seating areas, letting the cook to take part in conversations and socialize with family and friends while preparing the meal.

When planning your island, the first consideration is the space surrounding it. To keep traffic flowing smoothly in and out of the kitchen, allow at least 42 inches (105cm) between the island and surrounding cabinetry, furniture, and appliances.

Many islands have a raised, bar-height ledge for casual dining; however, opting for a contiguous surface can be more versatile in the long run. A large, level surface offers the flexibility to add additional seating for dining, set up a buffet style meal, or the extra space needed to spread out and work on a project.

When selecting a surface, think beauty and durability. Since the island is the focal point, this surface is the place to splurge on a showcase feature. For example, use solid stone and opt for elegant bevelled edges, or select beautifully textured hardwood. Because the island is often the busiest place in the home, perhaps choose a surface suitable for a variety of activities that will stand up to the demands of daily life.

If your plans call for a casual dining space at one end of the island, extending the countertop 12 to 18 inches (30 to 45cm) over the base will create ample legroom for people to sit comfortably.

To create a clean, symmetrical look in your kitchen, match the base of the island to the finish of the surrounding cabinets. To create a contrast, select a finish that is different, yet complements, the cabinets.

Make the most of this workspace by fitting it with well-planned storage and other features. Since the island generally anchors one end of the kitchen work triangle, use the side facing the cooking area to organize pots and pans, store spices, and place cutlery within easy reach. You might want to consider adding a pull-out cutting board as an extra work area.

On another side, build adjustable shelves for vegetable bins, cook book, or children's craft works. Or, include a small refrigerator, or perhaps a cabinet for glassware to create a convenient beverage center that might reduce foot traffic in the cooking zone when you are entertaining. To light the island from above, locate the lighting fixtures so they shine directly down, and not behind, the surface. Placing lighting for the island on dimmer switches means that one or two overhead pendant fittings can

provide the right lighting for activities ranging from casual dining and entertaining, to cooking, reading, and creating crafts.

Finally, add convenient electrical outlets on all sides of the island's cabinet base so you can use small appliances and a laptop computer while seated at this location.

Above This clean-lined, contemporary island serves as the main food preparation area in the large kitchen space. The unit features small and large drawers and cabinets, and has a practical, heat-resistant surface.

THE PERSONALIZED KITCHEN

You have done the research, determined your needs, set a realistic budget, and evaluated the options. Here comes the fun part: Personalizing your new kitchen with your favorite features. Now is the time to prioritize the items on your wish-list. Try as you might, no one can have it all; even those with the most generous budgets are faced with limitations. However, with thoughtful planning, each homeowner can incorporate the items that top the list, regardless of the size of their kitchen, or their pocketbook.

How? Simply by adding those features to the design first. Think of it this way. Creating a new kitchen is a wonderful opportunity to design a space to enjoy for years to come. The key to that enjoyment is to layer the kitchen with the features you love, and are practical for the way you live.

Begin the personalization process with a list of the top five "must-have" features. These are the non-negotiable choices. Is it a dual-fuel, six-burner commercial range with double ovens? Or two dishwashers and a built-in pantry? Maybe your dream is to have a laundry area that conveniently connects to the kitchen, or a wireless workstation placed in a convenient corner.

It could be that your wish-list has more to do with the style than the function of your kitchen. You might love the look of stainless appliances, exotic wood cabinetry, hand-forged drawer pulls, or a backsplash of glistening glass tiles. Your list might be made up of luxurious extras like an espresso bar, a wine refrigerator, a built-in pet food dispenser, or a refrigerated drawer that places cold drinks within easy reach of young children.

Regardless of what shape your dream takes, make those features the cornerstone of the new kitchen. Armed with the individual costs of these five features, and the plan of the layout, work out how to include them.

Often, homeowners make the mistake of playing it safe by going with kitchen designs that are more focused on the future resale of the home rather than the current requirements and desires. However, if you plan to remain in your home for at least the next ten to 15 years, it makes better sense to personalize your kitchen with features that suit your current needs, rather than those of a

Above A wide center island is personalized with a row of tiny drawers that hold herbs, dry goods and some cooking and serving utensils.

future buyer. Too often you hear stories of the buyer ripping out the new kitchen as soon as they take possession of a home, even if it was brand new.

This cornerstone approach offers a fail-safe formula for tailoring a space specific to your needs. It also helps you to remain focused when sifting through the endless array of design choices with which you will be faced. Setting priorities early in the process allows you to eliminate certain options from the start, either because they don't fit the way you want to use the kitchen, or because they really are too expensive.

The reality is that it may also mean letting go of less-important features or cutting back elsewhere in the kitchen design.

Spending more on integrated appliances might mean giving up custom cabinetry. Or vice versa.

Adding a large center island could mean sacrificing a sit-down dining area in the kitchen. If you make that decision, will it make a difference to the way the kitchen will work for you and the family?

If you take cooking seriously, you might want to include specific smaller drawers and chopping areas that make preparation easier, which means selecting the inside of the cabinetry with this in mind.

It is crucial to develop priorities based upon a thorough assessment of everybody's needs and desires. That way, you will to strike a good balance in your new kitchen.

Below Red lacquered cabinets personalize this space as do the built-in espresso machine and custom-concrete surfaces.

THE SMART KITCHEN

Appliance manufacturers are turning up the heat on kitchen technology, developing a new generation of features that add convenience, cut cooking times, and order our busy lives. Though many of these great gadgets are expensive, more and more high-tech timers, controls, integrated functions, and special settings will feature in mainstream appliances and home computers over the next few years. Here is a summary of what you can look forward to:

► Staying in touch with the office, or ordering groceries online, can be as close as your refrigerator, with technology that integrates cold food storage and internet communication. For about the price of a small car, choose a side-by-side refrigerator with a built-in screen for watching TV, accessing recipes, posting family messages, and storing favorite photos. The appliance refrigerates food with space-age efficiency—an interior drawer's thermostat is pre-programmed with settings such as quick chill and rapid thaw.

► Emerging technology also makes it possible to network appliances, home security, and room lighting from a flip-down screen installed beneath an upper cabinet. Watch DVD's, set timers, or send emails from a kitchen-worthy wireless keyboard that can be rinsed off with running water at the sink.

► Here is perhaps an even more appealing idea. Grind espresso beans or turn on the tea kettle before your toes touch the floor with the aid of a bedside touch screen that lets you operate appliances remotely.

Range combines refrigeration and roasting in one appliance. Pre-program the unit to slowly thaw foods for several hours before it automatically switches to a bake or roast setting, timed to your arrival home at the end of the day. Dinner is ready before you pull into the driveway.

You will be able to access hundreds of recipes (ingredients, instructions for step-by-step preparation, and nutritional information) from the internet via a microwave, which is programmed to take care of cooking times.

Kitchen networks will perform routine maintenance checks on appliances, keep tabs on grocery sell-by dates, place orders online when supplies are low, maintain the household schedule, send reminder emails, order flowers for a dinner party, or notify a family member when it is time to reorder prescription medication.

Opposite page, top
A flat-panel television installed on a motorized lift raises up and out of sight when it is not in use.

Opposite page, bottom
Wireless technology makes it possible for a cook to access recipes and emails without ever leaving the kitchen.

A MEDIA CENTER

Next to cooking and dining, television viewing ranks as the most common activity in multi-use kitchens. Factoring the entertainment system into plans at the start will ensure several people can share the space at one time with a minimum of noise.

Situate the television so it can be viewed from various places in the room. Built-in cabinets, with doors and drawers to conceal electric components, cords, and speakers prevent the television from becoming the focal point of the room when not in use. Look for retractable, swivelling television platforms for comfort viewing.

Sound quality is also important. Wiring the kitchen for separate audio zones lets people control the volume of music and television in these areas.

Add upholstered furnishings, drapes or carpeting, especially in kitchens with high ceilings, to absorb noise, eliminate echoes, and create a quality, pleasing sound to the ears.

T H E
P R A C T I C A L S

In this chapter, options for the floor, wall, and countertop surfaces are featured. Remember, style must be balanced with durability and low maintenance. Here, the pros and cons of both natural and manmade surfaces are presented to help you choose the right surface to set the tone and character of your new kitchen.

Right
Pale wood and pale cabinetry combine in this spacious and light-filled kitchen to produce smart heritage style.

WALL TREATMENTS

Choosing a wall treatment for your kitchen involves more than simply making a decorative statement to convey the style of the space. In busiest room of the home, durability and easy care are a must to keep the kitchen clean and looking its best for years to come.

Wall color is an inexpensive solution suitable for very high traffic areas and perfect for homes with young children. In the kitchen, apply washable acrylic paints in satin or gloss finishes that are easy to wipe down with soap and water. Always choose wall color with care, it is a dominant design element that can completely change the character of a space. Terra cotta tones, buttery yellows and shades of sage green convey comfort and warmth in the kitchen. More energetic colors like purple and orange stimulate the senses and can easily overpower the space, and the people in it. Also have a look at one of the new paint formulations that offer unique finishes for the kitchen. For example, turn an ordinary wall into a family-friendly message center or bulletin board with blackboard or magnetic paint. Simply tape off a portion of the wall and apply two coats of the paint to create a convenient place to post a schedule, leave important telephone numbers, or display favorite photos.

Wallpaper can hide a multitude of sins, especially if surfaces are flawed or uneven. However, constant exposure to heat and steam in the kitchen may cause even the sturdiest paper to peel over time. And, since what goes up must eventually come down, keep in mind that when it comes time to redecorate, removing wallpaper can be an arduous task. If you do opt for wallpaper in the kitchen, be sure to select a good quality vinyl or plastic coated "scrubbable" paper that wipes clean. And, unless someone in your household has considerable do-it-yourself experience, hire a professional paper hanger to do the job and ensure that seams and corners are expertly sealed.

If you like the look of wallpaper, but not the maintenance associated with it, consider

Left Continuing the countertop material on the backsplash and wall above the upper cabinets creates a smooth look and offers easy maintenance.

CEILINGS: WHAT'S UP

▶ KNOWN AS THE "FIFTH WALL" OF A ROOM, THE CEILING PROVIDES A NEW DESIGN OPPORTUNITY. ONE OF THE MOST SIGNIFICANT SHIFTS IN RESIDENTIAL ARCHITECTURE HAS BEEN TO INCREASE A ROOM'S VOLUME BY RAISING THE CEILING. IN HOMES WHERE SPACE LIMITATIONS PREVENT AN INCREASE IN SQUARE FOOTAGE OF A KITCHEN, ADDING HEIGHT AND NATURAL LIGHT TO A ROOM CAN CREATE THE ILLUSION OF A LARGER, MORE DRAMATIC SPACE.

▶ CHECK YOUR HOME'S ARCHITECTURAL STRUCTURE; INCREASING VOLUME MAY BE AS SIMPLE AS ELIMINATING A DROPPED CEILING TO UNCOVER EXPOSED BEAMS, PLANKS, OR TRUSSES THAT CAN ADD HEIGHT AND CHARACTER.

▶ IF RAISING THE CEILING IS NOT AN OPTION, INCREASE THE AMOUNT OF NATURAL LIGHT THROUGH A SKYLIGHT OR ROW OF CLERESTORY WINDOWS PLACED JUST BELOW THE CEILING LINE.

Above Shimmering glass wall tile complements the stainless steel cabinetry.The tile extends to the ceiling, wrapping the space in a sparkling layer of texture.

wall stencils. Easy to work with, stencils are available in an enormous range of designs to suit every style of kitchen. Simply start in one corner of the room and continue around using a repeating pattern to mimic the look of wallpaper for a fraction of the cost. Best of all, you can easily correct mistakes or paint over the pattern when you are ready to change the kitchen décor. Choose from basic, one color overall designs such as a garden lattice, two dimensional tone on tone patterns that add shadow and depth, or more elaborate overlays to create a custom *trompe l'oeile* design in the kitchen. Have a favorite saying or quote? Stencil manufacturers will create custom laser-cut templates for a small fee.

Wood panels, moldings and appliqués add instant character to kitchen walls.

Choose classic bead board to suggest a farmhouse feel, a formal chair rail for a more traditional tone, or intricate appliqués or medallions to convey Victorian charm. Wood, particularly when painted, is durable, easy to clean and renewable by sanding and repainting. In addition, applying wood paneling to kitchen walls builds-in a layer of soundproofing insulation that reduces noise and in the room.

FLOORING OPTIONS

Though choosing flooring that complements cabinetry and other design elements of the room is important, day-to-day care is of equal significance.

One important consideration is how resilient the material is underfoot. When standing for long periods of time, softer flooring, such as wood or linoleum, tends to be easier on the feet and back than the less-forgiving surfaces such as stone and tile. The best test of flooring is to try samples of several different materials at home for a few days to see how they stand up to foot traffic and how they feel beneath your feet.

From a design standpoint, flooring can unify or delineate a space. Using the same flooring material throughout a large room that contains a cooking zone as well as dining and informal seating areas will make the space appear more connected. Conversely, choosing contrasting flooring materials for different sections of the same room is means of subtly separating one function area from another. Also take into consideration the flooring in adjacent rooms to make sure there is a logical transition from one color or pattern to the next.

If remodelling, take into account the depth of your existing floor if you plan to add new material on top. In some cases, stripping old flooring is necessary to maintain a smooth transition between rooms.

Hardwood floors found elsewhere in the home can often be matched and continued into a remodeled kitchen or addition if you want to continue that style.

Use flooring to create a custom style statement in your new kitchen. For example, enhance ordinary hardwood by incorporating an Arts & Crafts-inspired inlay that pays quiet homage to the architectural heritage of the home. Or, you may want to play up a Mediterranean mood by adding hand-painted accent tiles to a terracotta floor. Linoleum lends itself particularly well to custom, computer-generated, laser-cut patterns and borders, and the natural beauty of stone adds rich texture to any room.

Browse the flooring showrooms for inspiration. You may find an application that will make your kitchen unique. Remember to take samples of cabinets, countertop, and backsplash materials to coordinate the color, pattern, and texture of flooring with the overall kitchen design. A summary of flooring options starts on the opposite page.

IN MOST SITUATIONS, FLOORING IS INSTALLED BEFORE CABINETS ARE SET IN PLACE. THE REASONING HERE IS THAT IT IS EASIER FOR FLOORING CONTRACTORS TO INSTALL ONE CONTIGUOUS SURFACE THAN IT IS TO WORK AROUND CABINET CORNERS AND EDGES. IF THIS IS THE CASE IN YOUR KITCHEN, BE SURE THAT YOUR CONTRACTOR PROTECTS THE NEW FLOOR FROM DAMAGE DURING THE REMAINDER OF THE PROJECT. A DURABLE LAYER OF CARDBOARD OR THICK PLASTIC SHEETING WILL WARD OFF NICKS, SCRAPES, AND SCUFF MARKS FROM CONSTRUCTION WEAR AND TEAR.

BAREFOOT COMFORT

▶ THOUGH NATURAL TILE AND STONE (SHOWN ABOVE) ARE VERSATILE AND DURABLE FLOORING MATERIALS, THEY CAN BE TOO COLD FOR COMFORT, ESPECIALLY IN CHILLIER CLIMATES. NEW ADVANCES IN RADIANT HEAT TECHNOLOGY, HOWEVER, HAVE THE CHANGED THE WAY THESE MATERIALS ARE USED IN LIVING SPACES.

▶ THE LATEST SYSTEMS, INSTALLED AS A THIN LAYER BETWEEN THE SUBFLOOR AND THE FLOORING MATERIAL, RADIATE A CLEAN, AMBIENT HEAT THAT WARMS UP COLD TILE AND STONE TO A COMFORTABLE TEMPERATURE IN MINUTES. THANKS TO THE HEAT-RETENTION PROPERTIES OF TILE AND STONE, THE FLOOR MAINTAINS ITS TEMPERATURE WITH A MINIMUM OF ENERGY. SEEK OUT SYSTEMS THAT OFFER PROGRAMMABLE THERMOSTATS TO CYCLE THE HEAT ON AND OFF AS NECESSARY THROUGHOUT THE DAY AND NIGHT.

Above Beautifully textured oak flooring wears well in high traffic areas. However, it must be protected from moisture with a sealant and may need re-sealing on a regular basis after a number of years.

HARDWOOD

Pros: Warm and elegant, wood grain adds texture underfoot. Milled in an assortment of tones, grain patterns, and plank widths to suit a range of kitchen styles, a wood floor is renewable and will stand up to decades of wear with the proper care. It may be sealed onsite, or installed in pre-finished planks.

Cons: Hardwoods are prone to water damage if exposed to moisture for extended periods of time. These floors require periodic sanding and resealing to restore finish and maintain good appearance. The surface may scratch and show signs of uneven wear in high traffic areas. Intricate designs, special cuts, and custom installations of hardwood floors can be costly.

Above Black and white linoleum tiles offer crisp, timeless character on a kitchen floor. Linoleum rarely shows signs of wear, even in high traffic areas.

LINOLEUM

Pros: Durable, linoleum floors actually improve with age and often last up to 50 years. Composed of all natural materials, linoleum is installed in sheets or squares that are easily configured to accommodate borders, inlays or custom designs. Because linoleum's color penetrates through the product, rather than just on the surface of the material, scratches and dents are less visible.

Cons: Requires substantial subfloor preparation and needs to be installed by a flooring professional who has experience working with the material. Since linoleum is comprised primarily of wood pulp, prolonged exposure to standing water, particularly at the seams, may cause the floor to warp or bubble. Periodic application of commercial grade floor wax is necessary to maintain sheen.

VINYL

Pros: Affordable and versatile, vinyl is readily available in an enormous range of colors and styles. The latest offerings include textured 'faux sisal' surfaces. In addition, vinyl is one of the least expensive flooring options and can be installed in a matter of hours. A soft surface, vinyl is comfortable when standing for long periods of time.

Cons: Easily scratched and more prone to damage than other types of flooring; must be replaced, rather than repaired when damage does occur. Because it is sold in long rolls, seams are often visible after installation. Brighter colors fade with prolonged exposure to sunlight and harsh detergents can dull the factory finish. Can shrink or pull over time.

TILE

Pros: Tile floors are durable, making them a good choice for high traffic areas like the kitchen. In addition, it is easy to repair or replace sections of the floor if damage does occur. Relatively inexpensive when compared with other materials, tile is readily available in a seemingly endless array of shapes, sizes, colors and is easy to customize to any number of design applications.

Cons: Tile surfaces are hard and can be cold, depending upon climate. Grout lines trap dirt, easily discolor and require ongoing maintenance. Glazed ceramic tile, though extremely durable, is slippery when wet. Non-glazed clay tile is porous and prone to staining.

LAMINATE

Pros: Laminate offers good looks, durability and easy care. Made up of a solid core beneath a realistic photograph of wood or stone and topped with a strong, clear plastic layer. Laminate looks like a natural product, but is in fact the same manmade material used on countertops since the 1950s. Stands up to heavy traffic and cleans up with simple soap and water, and is a good choice for busy households with children and pets.

Cons: Engineered products lack the character of authentic hardwood or stone. Depending upon they quality of the subfloor, laminate can give off a hollow sound when walked upon. Though laminate is safe for most kitchen applications, standing water or leaks could cause warping if moisture seeps beneath the top layer of the product.

BAMBOO

Pros: A relative newcomer to the residential flooring market, bamboo is quickly gaining favor with kitchen designers and homeowners. Considered an environmentally friendly alternative to hardwood, bamboo is harder than oak and offers great design versatility. Eco-friendly; bamboo plants take just three years to mature. May be installed over other flooring and is easy to maintain.

Cons: Quality can vary. All bamboo is harvested from controlled forests in China. To ensure the best quality and the highest grade bamboo, purchase materials from reputable dealers that offer at least a fifteen year warranty on installed flooring.

Right Pieces of recycled glass surrounded by marble tile creates a multicolored mosaic border.

SUSTAINABLE STYLE

► ADD CHARM AND TEXTURE TO A KITCHEN WITH BUILDING MATERIALS SUCH AS ANTIQUE WOOD, STONE AND TILES SALVAGED FROM DEMOLISHED BUILDINGS.

USE RECLAIMED MATERIALS EXCLUSIVELY, OR BLEND THEM WITH NEW MATERIALS TO ADD INTEREST. MAKE A BORDER OUT OF HISTORIC PAVERS RECOVERED FROM A CENTURY-OLD ROW HOUSE, OR INSTALL ANTIQUE PINE FLOORING FROM A NEW ENGLAND FACTORY IN A COUNTRY KITCHEN.

SINCE MOST SALVAGED GOODS ARE SOLD "AS-IS", MAKE SURE ROOM MEASUREMENTS ARE ACCURATE AND INSPECT ALL MATERIALS BEFORE YOU BUY.

ALSO, IF YOU DO NOT FIND WHAT YOU WANT ON THE FIRST VISIT, CHECK BACK FREQUENTLY AS INVENTORY CHANGES FROM DAY TO DAY. SHOP FOR SALVAGED MATERIALS ONLINE, OR OBTAIN REFERRALS FROM LOCAL BUILDERS AND ARCHITECTS.

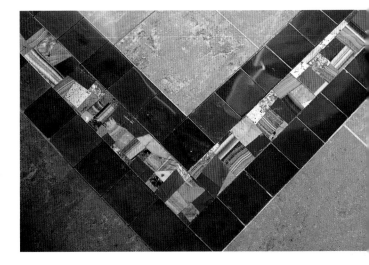

COUNTERTOPS

From the natural beauty of polished stone to the design versatility and affordability of laminate, there is no shortage of textural choices when selecting this all-important design feature.

Next to flooring, countertops experience more wear and tear than any other feature of the kitchen. For that reason alone, choosing a hard-wearing surface that can stand up to the demands of daily life, while still maintaining its appearance, should be the primary consideration when selecting a material for your countertop.

The selection process means balancing style, practicality, and budget. The first step in the process is to match each surface with the overall design, then narrow your options to two or three different materials that complement both the architectural tone and cabinetry style. From there, consider the durability and maintenance requirements of these choices and decide if the one you want will stand up to the way your use the kitchen. Although every surface requires some routine care, certain types of materials are more prone to stains and scratches, or require extra care or special sealants to preserve their appearance.

The second step requires consideration of long term wear and tear. Some surfaces, such as butcher block, have a timeless quality that actually improves with age, taking on a rich patina that adds character to the kitchen. Consider how a countertop you choose today might look in ten or 20 years.

Finally, compare the cost. There is a tremendous difference between higher-priced materials such as stone and solid surfacing, and the more affordable alternatives such as laminate. When pricing a selection, check to be sure that the amount you are quoted includes installation, not just the price of materials. Also keep in mind that the cost of custom work, such as detailed edges, quickly adds up. If cost is your primary consideration, straight edges and simple detailing are the most economical choices.

Mixing and matching two or more surfaces in the various task zones of a kitchen adds textural interest to the space and also maximizes kitchen function. For example, a kitchen might feature a granite island, a stainless steel sink surround, and a butcher block preparation area all within the same cooking zone.

When planning the kitchen, include at least one 36" (90cm) contiguous countertop. The material should have a smooth surface, be easy to clean, and be suitable for a variety of culinary tasks including chopping, mixing, and rolling dough.

Also consider the height of the countertop, as previously suggested. The current standard is to install all surfaces at a height of 36" (90cm). However, raising or lowering by a few inches to accommodate the individual needs of your household will greatly improve comfort in the kitchen without adversely affecting the future resale value of your home (see Universal Design, page 00).

Below Plastic laminate gets an updated look by way of a countertop application that curves to form a breakfast bar.

COUNTERTOP OPTIONS

Countertops are the final feature of a kitchen design and are added during the construction. It is important to factor in the required lead time when planning your space. Solid-slab surfaces are custom made from a template drawn after the cabinets have been installed and may take from six to eight weeks to complete. A laminate surface has a turnaround time of about two weeks. Tile and wood surfaces can generally be installed as soon as the cabinets are set into place.

GRANITE

Pros: An extremely durable material, granite is naturally waterproof and stain resistant making it an ideal surface for cooking and food preparation. The color and quality can vary dramatically depending upon slab and type of granite selected. Smaller veins in the slab generally indicate a more durable surface.

Cons: It is expensive, particularly if curved corners and intricate edges are added to the slab. There can be a long lead time from ordering to completion and this may delay the completion of the kitchen. Also, granite can create a cold feeling in the kitchen, and a piece of granite may require reinforced base cabinets to support the extra weight.

BUTCHER BLOCK

Pros: Warm, resilient, and reasonably priced, butcher block is a natural, renewable cooking surface ideal for chopping fruit, vegetables and meat. Variations and subtle texture provide character. If not to be used as a cutting surface, a butcher block may be sealed with a food-grade lacquer to preserve its smooth finish.

Cons: Prolonged exposure to water can warp the wood, which makes it a less-practical choice of surface to use as the sink surround. If the butcher block surface is used for chopping and cutting, it must periodically be sanded and conditioned with a food-safe mineral oil to prevent the wood grain from drying out.

Above
Square corners and deep edges give a Carrera marble countertop a sleek look. Electrical outlets on the side of the island are hidden by a panel when not in use.

SOLID SURFACE

Pros: Available in a broad spectrum of colors and texture, solid surface countertops are synthetic smooth, seamless workspaces. They may be further customized with inlays, decorative edges, integrated sinks, and backsplashes. In addition, a solid surface is waterproof, scratch resistant, and low maintenance.

Cons: A solid surface can be expensive; the cost is comparable to granite. Also, the synthetic material can burn if exposed to intense heat. Deep scratches or damage that cannot be buffed out may have to be professionally sanded or patched to restore the surface.

LAMINATE

Pros: Affordable and easy to maintain, laminate offers an enormous range of colors, textures, and patterns, including some that mimic the look of natural stone. Special edge treatments customize the application. Laminates have a short lead time and can be manufactured quickly.

Cons: This type of surface can warp if water penetrates beneath the surface and it is prone to scratching, and therefore is not suitable for use as a chopping surface. Hot pots and pans can melt the surface. If damaged, laminate is nearly impossible to repair and you may have to replace the countertop if it is badly damaged by a domestic accident.

Left   Tongue and groove maple visually separates the central workspace from cabinets on the periphery of the kitchen.

Bottom   Marble makes a lustrous and durable kitchen surface, but it is not maintenance-free. Periodic sealing is required to prevent staining from coffee, wine, and oil.

STAINLESS STEEL:

Pros: A commercial-grade surface frequently used by professionals, it is extremely durable, heat-proof, and nearly indestructible. Stainless steel is a good choice for serious cooks. Its smooth, non-corrosive surface makes it easy to sanitize and maintain. Stainless steel scratches easily. However, daily wear and tear can create a desirable patina over the years. It is available with a shiny or a brushed matte finish.

Cons: A stainless-steel countertop can be noisy. homeowners should consider adding insulation underneath to muffle sound. Though the material is inexpensive, custom applications can greatly increase the price. Stainless is not suitable for use as a chopping and cutting surface since it will dull knife blades.

TILE

Pros: Durable, heat-resistant and versatile, tile lends itself to any number of design applications. Granite tiles offer the attributes of the stone for a fraction of the cost of a solid slab surface. Special edge and border tiles create a custom look for countertops, edges, and backsplashes. Individual tiles also are easy to replace if they are damaged.

Cons: Grouting is prone to stains and cracks and requires regular cleaning and sealing to maintain appearance. Surface seams may make cleaning up difficult and tiles may crack or chip if heavy items are dropped onto them. Also, the cost can add up quickly depending upon which materials or edge treatments you select, and the intricacy of the design.

EDGE NAMES

▶ SQUARE ALSO KNOWN AS PENCIL EDGE. THE MOST COMMONLY USED AND LEAST-EXPENSIVE EDGE TREATMENT.

▶ BULLNOSE CREATED BY CURVING THE MATERIAL OVER THE EDGE OF THE COUNTER. IN THE KITCHEN?

▶ SANDWICH MADE BY FUSING LAYERS OF MATERIAL TOGETHER. MOST COMMONLY USED IN LAMINATE EDGES WHERE A LAYER OF WOOD GLUED BETWEEN TWO SLABS OF LAMINATE CREATES A DETAILED EDGE.

▶ OGEE A CONCAVE, 'S-SHAPED' TREATMENT USED ON STONE COUNTERTOPS. A COSTLY EDGE TREATMENT.

CONCRETE

Pros: Natural beauty and an earthy texture create a custom countertop. Design options are unlimited since concrete can have a sleek, streamlined appearance, can take on the look of polished stone, may be dyed to match surrounding room elements, or imbedded with glass gems, leaves or shells to create a unique finish.

Cons: Using concrete is labor intensive because countertops are poured on site. Expensive, it can be pricier than stone. Base cabinets must be reinforced to support the weight, and surfaces require resealing once or twice a year. Concrete can stain and crack, although some people find these imperfections enhance, rather than detract from, the appearance.

CABINETRY

Whether you prefer the character of warm wood or lean more toward the sleek elegance of stainless steel, the cabinets you select set the style of the kitchen. Learn about this key design feature; then choose from an array of fabulous finishes, divine details, and custom configurations to help you create your one-of-a-kind kitchen.

Right Dark wood cabinetry makes a strong design statement in this wonderful open-plan kitchen created for a family lifestyle.

KITCHEN CABINETS

Cabinetry creates the first impression when you enter a kitchen and is the most important design element in conveying style. Whether your kitchen has a clean-lined, contemporary look, or evokes an elegant, European farmhouse feel will depend upon the type of cabinet you select.

Not surprisingly, cabinets are generally the largest expense incurred when creating a new kitchen. Depending upon the style, finish and features you choose, cabinet costs can quickly add up to more than half of the total kitchen budget. Because of these design and cost considerations, the selection of cabinets is, for many kitchen designers, a logical starting point in the planning process.

Though kitchen cabinets are available in a seemingly endless array of shapes, sizes, functions, and finishes, they fall into three categories: Custom, stock, and semi-custom.

Left A custom-built end cabinet richly detailed with furniture trim, open storage shelves and rows of tiny spice drawers imparts an air of Old World elegance in this traditional kitchen.

Custom cabinets are those built specifically for your kitchen. They are designed to fit the space and outfitted with features and finishes selected by the homeowner. Since they are built to specification, custom cabinets have the longest lead time, typically it is about three months from when you place the order to when the kitchen is installed, and consequently they are the most expensive of any other type of cabinet. On the plus side, custom-built cabinets offer superior craftsmanship, excellent quality and an unlimited range of options and features.

Semi-custom cabinets feature the best of both worlds: design flexibility and superior quality. Semi-custom cabinets are factory made and can typically arrive within a matter of weeks. Most manufacturers offer a wide range of options and modifications that enable their products to conform to just about any kitchen style and layout. This offers you a greater design freedom and gives you the ability to create a kitchen with unique character and detail for less than the cost of custom cabinetry.

Though the choice of cabinet style and quality is largely driven by budget, occasionally other factors come into play. For example, the size and space limitations of remodeling a kitchen within an existing blueprint could leave custom-built cabinetry as the only choice to fit the configuration.

Below The sleek profile of minimally detailed frameless doors and drawers define the contemporary tone of the space, and bring into focus the wood's grain and texture.

FRESH FACED

▶ IF YOUR CURRENT CABINETS ARE DATED YET STRUCTURALLY SOUND, CONSIDER REFACING, RATHER THAN REPLACING, THEM. THIS WILL COST ABOUT ONE-THIRD OF THE PRICE OF NEW CABINETS. HERE IS HOW THE PROCESS WORKS:

▶ A LICENSED KITCHEN CONTRACTOR REMOVES CABINET DOORS, DRAWER FRONTS, HARDWARE, AND HINGES. NEXT, A LAYER OF HARDWOOD OR LAMINATE VENEER IS FUSED TO THE EXISTING CABINET FRAMES TO CREATE A FRESH FINISH. FINALLY, NEW DOORS AND DRAWERS, HARDWARE, AND HINGES ARE INSTALLED. EXPECT THE PROCESS TO TAKE ABOUT A WEEK.

Stock cabinets are mass-produced in standard sizes designed to fit most standard kitchen designs and are available in a limited selection of decorative options, door styles, and hardware. Available at home-improvement centers, stock cabinets are reasonably priced. However, construction quality varies greatly from one manufacturer to then next and it pays to visit several stores and compare prices before purchasing. For durability and sturdiness, choose cabinets with plywood veneer frames and particleboard shelving faced with melamine or laminate.

CABINET STYLE

Not long ago, rows of boxy cabinets stacked one on top
of the other were the uninspired common denominator
of a basic kitchen design. Thankfully, concepts have
changed for the better.

Above Lit
from within,
these frosted
glass doors
create visual
interest in this
set of modern
cabinets.

Kitchen cabinets are the key ingredient in
creating the architectural character that
defines the overall tone of the kitchen. With
the old design rules relaxed, a marvelous
mixed medley of cabinet shapes, styles, and
finishes has emerged. It is not uncommon to
see two or three different door styles and
wood finishes beautifully blended within the
same space. Where a monotonous row of
flat-paneled wall cabinets all set at the same
height might once have set the standard, a
variation of height and depth of the same
cabinets now sets the style.

Use your home's architectural
influence as a guide when selecting
cabinetry. Repeating design elements found
elsewhere in the home visually connects the
kitchen to the surrounding space. A gracious
arched entrance might be echoed on a
cabinet door panel; the lustrous wood grain
of dining room furnishings repeated on a
center island.

Choose the color and finish of a
cabinet with equal care. Keep in mind two
design rules: Dark colors absorb light and
make spaces feel smaller; lighter shades and
glass doors reflect light and visually enlarge
a room.

Maintenance is another factor to
consider when choosing a cabinet finish. In
bustling households with children and pets,
a low-sheen, matte finish that "conceals"
fingerprints would be a better choice than a
high-gloss finish that requires constant
cleaning. Mixing colors and finishes of
cabinetry is one way to add visual interest,
and possibly save money. Consider an
expensive hand-rubbed finish or exotic wood
veneer to showcase upper cabinets which
tend to be more visible, and select a less
costly, complementary color or finish for base
cabinets which are generally less visible.

Above In this large, traditional and hand-crafted kitchen, the staggered height of the custom cabinets, its full overlay doors, molding, trim, and lattice detail convey absolute luxury.

CABINET TERMS

▶ **FACE-FRAME:** A CABINET STYLE THAT FEATURES A ONE- TO TWO-INCH HARDWOOD FRAME VISIBLE AROUND THE FRONT FACE OF THE CABINET BOX.

▶ **FLUSH-INSET:** DOORS AND DRAWERS FIT WITHIN THE CABINET FRAME TO CREATE A SEAMLESS SURFACE.

▶ **FRAMELESS:** (ALSO KNOWN AS FULL OVERLAY.) DOORS AND DRAWER FRONTS FIT FLUSH AND OVERLAY TO EDGE OF THE CABINET BOX.

▶ **UNFITTED:** FREESTANDING PIECES THAT MAY BE MOVED AROUND THE KITCHEN AND ARE NOT ATTACHED TO A WALL.

▶ **FITTED:** THIS REFERS TO PERMANENTLY INSTALLED CABINET BOXES.

▶ **EXPOSED HINGES:** VISIBLE HARDWARE PLACED ON THE OUTSIDE OF THE CABINET DOOR, THEY OFTEN COORDINATE WITH HARDWARE TO CREATE DECORATIVE DETAILS.

▶ **CONCEALED HINGES:** ATTACHED TO DOORS ON THE INSIDE OF THE CABINET, THESE GIVE A CLEAN-LINED LOOK.

▶ **SOFFIT:** THE SPACE BETWEEN THE TOP OF THE CABINET AND THE CEILING.

▶ **TOE--KICK:** THE RECESS AT THE BASE OF THE CABINET THAT ENABLES A PERSON TO STAND CLOSE ENOUGH TO THE COUNTER TO WORK COMFORTABLY.

Left This kitchen, designed by Mark Wilkinson, uses sparkling glass, brushed stainless steel, and the chocolate tones of natural walnut as key styling notes. The deep-etched glass panels provide added detail. Floor-level lighting creates the illusion that the furniture floats above the floor. The plinth has been increased in height and is deeply recessed. The glass-topped table, lit from below, is incorporated into the island. Adjacent the seating area is a rack for magazines and books.

KNOBS, PULLS, HANDLES
HINGES AND DRAWER SLIDES

Think of knobs, pulls, handles, and hinges as jewelry for cabinets. With thousands of decorative styles in stores, selecting the right hardware can be a delightful treasure hunt. This small item is a hardworking detail that can form the first impression of your kitchen.

When doing the budget, bear in mind that an average-sized layout can require as many as 40 to 50 pieces of hardware. If you select simple inexpensive designs, the cost can remain reasonable; however, if you opt for pricy, intricate shapes, the cost can rise.

Narrow the hardware options down to two to three styles that convey the look you want to establish. A sense of proportion between hardware and cabinet is more than essential. Handles or pulls that dominate the door or drawer front will look unattractive. A clunky design will detract from elegance and be hard on your hands. A handle must be easy to grab with both wet and dry hands; also, select a style that won't catch your ring finger, or your nails. Sharp corners can cut, so look for more rounded designs.

If your kitchen cabinets are traditional, consider antique copper, pewter, glass, or porcelain knobs and pulls. Perhaps accentuate contemporary cabinets with bold, geometric-shaped hardware made of modern materials, sculpted metal shapes, or sleek brushed stainless steel forms.

Make a statement that connects the kitchen to its environment. Use a metal twig drawer pull in a cabin retreat kitchen; a carved cactus handle in a desert home, or sea-glass knobs in a seaside kitchen.

Above A variety of polished metal bow-tie-inspired drawer pulls and handles dress up a smartly-styled custom-built kitchen.

Top Sturdy European hinges, typically used on face frame and full overlay doors, are fully concealed within the frame. The hinges adjust to align the doors.

Above Sculpted metal pulls contrast with warm wood cabinetry and echo the kitchen's straight edges.

HINGES

Hinge style is dictated by the type of cabinet. Frameless, or full overlay cabinets where the door fits flush with the cabinet box, require concealed hinges that need not match the knob or pull on the outside.

Hinges on face-frame and flush-inset cabinets are exposed, and must be coordinated with other cabinet hardware.

The size and number of hinges you will need per cabinet is determined by the door's dimension and weight.

Smaller, lightweight doors need just two hinges, but solid wood or full overlay doors that measure more than 40" (100cm) in height and weigh over 20lbs (about 9kg) require a minimum of three to four.

Cabinet hardware is not the area to skimp on quality. Investing in quality hardware ensures that the cabinet knobs, pulls, hinges, and handles will withstand the daily demands of a well-used kitchen. Also, because hardware styles frequently change, buy a few extra pieces to eliminate the need to change the hardware throughout the entire kitchen if one or two handles do wear out.

DRAWER SLIDES

The standard drawer slide produced by most manufacturers is a single, center-mounted slide that supports a minimum weight. Other options, such as heavy-duty, dual-mounted slides that support both sides of the drawer are considered an upgrade by kitchen companies, both in quality and cost.

Investing in durable glides, drawer stops, full-extension slides that reveal 3" to 4" (7.5cm to 10cm) more of drawer space, and self-closing mechanisms are extras that improve the overall functioning of a kitchen.

STORAGE

Efficient storage systems are the backbone of a well-designed kitchen. In this chapter, you will find some of the newest design options to help make your kitchen run smoothly. See for yourself how smart storage solutions combine practicality with style in all price brackets.

Right Stainless steel drawers with wide easy-to-grip handles, glide open for quick access to cookware stored close to the range.

KITCHEN STORAGE

Storage is the most important feature in determining the efficiency of your kitchen. At the planning stage, homeowners should spend at least as much time considering the inside of the cabinets as they do the outside.

Setting up storage systems for non-perishable food, spices, small appliances, cookware, cutlery, and dinnerware eliminates clutter and sets the stage for a well-organised space that runs smoothly.

Planning storage is a two-step process. Begin by designating specific activity zones within the kitchen for cooking, baking, food preparation and cleaning up, then evaluate each zone individually to incorporate features that fit those tasks.

Use your current kitchen as a starting point. Consider the storage systems that function well and, rather than re-inventing the wheel, duplicate the features that work, while modifying those that do not. Take stock of your kitchen contents to determine the best placement of specific items within the space, which will ensure every item has a home.

Reserve the most accessible storage for everyday items such as cookware and cutlery, and place these items close to where they will be used. Store less-frequently-used objects, such as your fine china or seasonal serving pieces, in cabinets on the periphery of the kitchen.

For practicality and future resale of your property, every kitchen should have a basic storage capacity that is flexible enough

Below A base cabinet has been transformed into a charming cart to roll out when it is tea time. The wheels are hidden; the cart also has fold-out sides for extra tea-cup space.

to suit most households. Beyond that, plan on personalizing your kitchen with the storage features suited to your style of cooking, dining and entertaining style.

Below A combination of open shelves, wire racks, small canisters, and see-through bins organize coffee, tea, and spices in a small cabinet.

OPEN SHELVING

OPTING FOR OPEN SHELVING, RATHER THAN CLOSED CABINETS, IS A PRACTICAL CONSIDERATION.

▶ ELIMINATING DOORS INCREASES USABLE STORAGE SPACE AND CAN DRAMATICALLY CUT YOUR MATERIAL COSTS.

▶ PROFESSIONAL CHEFS SAY THAT OPEN SHELVES PROVIDE EASY ACCESS TO ESSENTIALS, SAVING TIME AND MINIMIZING MOVEMENT.

▶ BACKLIT GLASS SHELVES CAN DISPLAY A COLLECTION OF POTTERY.

▶ OPEN SHELVES FITTED WITH WICKER BASKETS AND BINS MAKE A PRACTICAL STORAGE PLACE FOR FRESH PRODUCE BECAUSE THEY ALLOW FRESH AIR TO CIRCULATE.

▶ CARVE SHELVES OUT OF A LITTLE-USED CORNER OF AN ISLAND ORGANIZE COOK BOOK OR TO KEEP CHILDREN'S CRAFT SUPPLIES HANDY.

▶ ITEMS STORED ON OPEN SHELVES ARE MORE EXPOSED TO KITCHEN SOIL AND AIRBORNE GREASE PARTICLES. TO MINIMIZE THE EFFECTS, LOCATE SHELVES AS FAR AWAY FROM THE COOKING ZONE AS POSSIBLE. TAKE SPECIAL CARE TO PROTECT DELICATE, OR FRAGILE, ITEMS.

THE PANTRY

Keep the kitchen organised and clutter-free with the addition of a pantry. Thanks to the introduction of space-saving, fold-out pantry systems, even the smallest kitchen can benefit from improved organization.

Opposite page In this sculpted kitchen made by craftsmen, the corner unit acts a pantry. Its curved doors bring a soft edge to the corner.

Pantries fall into three categories: The cupboard pantry, or any unit that is incorporated into cabinetry; the essential pantry, a closet-sized space situated close to the cooking area, and the traditional butler's pantry, a separate room located between the kitchen and the formal dining room.

Stationed within the cooking area, cupboard pantries are ideal for storing cookware, utensils, dry ingredients, or even small appliances. This type of pantry, ideal for small kitchens where space is scarce, may be a pull-out unit beneath the counter or a larger fold-out unit built into a floor-to-ceiling unit.

Inside the cupboard, the space is customized according to the items that will be stored. Options include drawer dividers for utensils, adjustable shelving for glassware or non-perishable foods, bins for flour, rice and sugar, and racks for spices, and even space for kitchen linens.

The essential pantry is either a walk-in (a deep, closet-like space), or a step-in (a wide shallow space lined with open shelving). Ideally, essential pantries are located close enough to the cooking area to be convenient but far enough away to be unaffected by changing kitchen temperatures. This type of pantry includes non-perishable food storage as well as enough space to store small appliances, china, serving pieces, vegetable bins, bottled-water storage, and wines (if you do not have a wine cellar or wine chiller). Because these spaces tend to be dark, good lighting is crucial to the function of the essential pantry. Adding a light that automatically switches on and off when the door opens and closes makes it easier to quickly locate items.

The butler's pantry is a service area situated in a passageway between the kitchen and the formal dining area. In addition to storage for dishes and glassware, and counter space for staging meals, the butler's pantry may include a small refrigerator, dishwasher, or wine cellar. Because of its proximity to the entertaining area, more emphasis is placed on the design of the butler's pantry. Many homeowners choose to continue the same cabinetry used in the kitchen, add glass cabinets to display china, and special lighting.

If lack of space or budget prevents you from building a formal butler's pantry, consider adding a small cabinet and counter to a corner of the formal dining room area as a multi-use space that may be used as a bar, buffet, or extra storage.

ACCESSORIES

Once you have determined what you will be storing, and where, customize cabinet interiors with one of several accessory options that support the storage function. For example, a base cabinet beneath a cooktop is an obvious spot for storing cookware.

Here, consider incorporating heavy-duty roll out drawers that are sturdy enough to support extra weight and deep enough to hold a variety of pots and pans. Adding full extension slides to the drawer adds an additional 4" (10cm) of usable space and makes contents fully visible without you having to bend down.

If you prefer uncluttered countertops, adding pop-up stands to a cabinet for the toaster, coffee-maker, blender, and mixer allows easy access to small appliances but hides them when they are not in use.

Serious cooks might consider adapting drawers located next to the range with a built-in spice tray to store seasonings, or a cutlery rack to hold knives at the proper angle to prevent dulling. In addition to these features, consider these options when customizing your kitchen:

PLATE RACKS

Added to upper cabinets, or open shelving, plate racks feature individual slots for storing dinnerware vertically. In addition to organizing the kitchen, the racks can also prevent chips and scratches on your china.

RECYCLING AND TRASH BINS

Pullout bins built into base cabinets sort and collect kitchen waste. Though trash bins are best located beneath or next to the sink, placing them outside of the busy work triangle can free up valuable storage space.

Opposite page Full extension drawers in this base cabinet, fitted with heavy-duty stainless steel glides, provide versatile storage.

Right Custom stemware racks installed in an upper cabinet nearly triples the amount of useful space.

Below left A drawer situated close to the preparation zone features a collection of cooking utensils in a custom-made unit.

Below right In this compact kitchen a top-hinged door swings up to reveal a rack thatkeeps countertops clear by air drying clean dishesdirectly above the sink.

TAMBOUR STORAGE

Also known as an "appliance garage", these units store frequently used small appliances at counter level by concealing them behind a roll down door. If you decide to incorporate one into your kitchen, make sure to add an electrical outlet to the wall inside the space.

THE BAKING CENTER

Group baking necessities together by adapting a base cabinet to include moisture proof bins for flour and sugar, a pop-up stand for the mixer, and a pullout marble slab for rolling pastry.

WINE RACK

Replace a narrow base cabinet with wine storage. Locate in a cool, dry area of the kitchen away from the oven, the range, and away from direct sunlight.

WICKER VEGETABLE BINS

Sliding wicker baskets installed beneath the countertop provides a practical place for fresh fruits and vegetables in the kitchen and enables fresh air to circulate around produce.

ADJUSTABLE SHELVES

Opting for adjustable, rather than fixed shelves, increases storage options and builds more flexibility into the kitchen. Also consider purchasing an extra set of shelves to increase storage capacity and recover space in cabinets where smaller items are stored.

If either space or budget constraints limit your choices of built-in accessories, consider an open storage idea, for example, a pot rack that suspends cookware from the ceiling over the range or island. Pot racks are available in a range of sizes through restaurant suppliers, kitchen retailers, or metal crafters. They range in price from about $100 (£55) for a basic stainless steel rack to several hundred dollars for a big, hand-forged, copper-plated design outfitted with hooks and lighting.

Evaluate your kitchen to work out the various locations that may be easily and inexpensively fitted with flexible storage features. For example, you could install a spice rack along the backsplash to turn a purely decorative area into functional space. Alternatively, you could add a magnetic strip to the same space to make a convenient storage unit for cooking utensils.

Hang cookware lids from pegboard attached to the inside of cabinet doors, or add a series of sturdy hooks to turn the back of a kitchen door into a broom storage area.

If you have high ceilings in a small kitchen, select cabinets that reach the ceiling and buy a pair of small steps to access the top shelf when necessary.

Above This floor to ceiling glass and wood unit is a luxurious touch in a large modern kitchen. It is ideal for displaying a precious collection of dinnerware or glassware and is adjacent the kitchen's work areas so it can be easily accessed.

INSIDE INFO

Top left Built into a base cabinet, these small stainless steel storage units are for spices and other dry ingredients.

Above Handy recipe drawers are recessed into a small decorative column on the countertop. Below is a drawer for cooking utensils.

Left Pull-out pantries make the most of narrow kitchen spaces. This rack extends fully.

Above Installed at counter level, a pull-out rack is tucked behind a corbel and places spices and seasonings within easy reach of nearby baking and cooking zones.

Right, top Tambour storage units keep countertops clear by concealing small electric appliances such as toasters, coffee-making machines, blenders,, and juicers behind a sliding, shutter-type door.

Right, bottom This handy wire rack affixed to the back of a cabinet door holds a colorful assortment of plastic container lids.

LIGHTING

In the modern multi-functional central living space, a well-designed lighting plan is crucial as support to a variety of tasks and activities. This chapter asks you to think about how you use the kitchen, explains the basics of lighting, which light bulb is best for the situation, and how to transform the mood in the kitchen at the flick of a discreet switch.

Right Natural lighting floods the space during the day. The glass-fronted cabinets above the countertop feature fixtures on dimmer switches that serve as accent lighting at night.

GETTING WIRED

Since electrical wiring takes place in the early stages of building and remodeling, having a lighting plan in place before work begins will prevent unnecessary delays once building work begins.

In modern open floor plans, where cooking, dining, homework, reading and relaxing can all take place within the same kitchen space, a well-designed lighting scheme should support each of the room's functions and create a subtle backdrop for the full range of room activities.

Since lighting requirements differ from one kitchen to the next, perhaps consult a lighting professional early in the planning process to ensure a customized plan tailored to your room's layout, the amount of natural light, the architectural features and the specific work zones.

Also consider the types of materials used in the kitchen when selecting the lighting fixtures. For instance, the reflective qualities of stainless steel and certain high-sheen cabinet finishes generate a glare that can be neutralized with certain types of lighting. If you have choosen a matt cabinetry finish, you might want to boost the lighting there.

Choosing the right type of lighting is only half of the challenge; the proper placement of fixtures within the room is every bit as crucial. Precise placement is critical because here, even a few inches (a few centimeters) off may mean the difference between a well-lit kitchen designed for cooking, dining, and entertaining, and a gloomy, unappealing space cast in the wrong type of shadow. In addition, correcting lighting mistakes once the kitchen is complete can be costly and disruptive.

A good lighting plan will include a combination of ambient, task and accent lighting. Following is a brief introduction to the types of lighting available.

AMBIENT LIGHTING

Ambient (or overall) lighting softly illuminates the entire room and is generally the first type of light turned on when you enter the room. A common mistake made in many kitchens is the assumption that a single, overhead light placed in the center of the room will suffice for a variety of activities. Though ambient lighting typically generates enough light to comfortably move about the room, it lacks the intensity required for everyday tasks like food preparation, cooking, reading, or working at the kitchen table.

TASK LIGHTING

The next step in devising a lighting scheme is to ensure that each work area has adequate light for performing specific tasks. The best choice is downlighting that shines directly onto the work surface. Task lights may include under-cabinet fixtures, pendants, track lights, or cans recessed into the ceiling. Again, proper placement is the key to ensuring light is centered on, and not behind, work surfaces.

Adjustable track lighting offers flexibility to accommodate a number of cooks, as well as and the ability to direct light where it is needed most. Pendant lights suspended over an island or long stretch of countertop are another good choice as long as they are placed low enough to cast sufficient light onto the work surface (but high enough so you do not hit your head).

ACCENT LIGHTING

This type of lighting sets the mood of the room, highlights a specific architectural feature, or creates a focal point. Accent lighting also adds drama, creates character, or directs attention to a piece of artwork or special display. In open kitchens decorative lighting is a subtle means of delineating different areas of the room. Use accent lighting inside glass paneled cabinets, beneath upper cabinets to illuminate the backsplash, or tucked inside a soffit to draw the eye up and visually heighten the room. When entertaining, use soft accent lighting to direct guests away from kitchen work areas, and into social areas of the room.

Above Recessed ceiling lights on dimmer switches serve as task lighting when turned up and accent lighting when turned low. Back-lit upper cabinets create graceful silhouettes behind glass doors.

LIGHT BULBS

The type of bulb you select for kitchen fixtures has tremendous impact on the quality of light, as well as the amount of energy used to light the space. Take the time to familiarize yourself with the options to choose the best light bulb for the fixture and the task.

INCANDESCENT

Incandescent light bulbs, also known as A-style bulbs, are the most widely available, the least expensive to buy, and have a standard thread that fits most lighting fixtures. Available in several different wattages, are easy to use with dimmer switches and produce a warm light that is flattering to skin tones and food. However, they tend to be the least energy efficient type of bulb, have the shortest life, and may require frequent replacement in high use areas of the home such as the kitchen.

FLUORESCENT

Fluorescent lights still suffer from an image problem in the minds of many consumers. Often equated with harsh overhead lighting that did little to improve the look or feel of a space, the outdated fluorescent tubes have been replaced with today's Compact Fluorescent bulbs. Designed with the same thread as incandescent bulbs, compact fluorescents use a fraction of the energy and burn hundreds of hours longer. CFL bulbs are more expensive, however longer burn time and lower energy consumption are trade-offs worth considering. One drawback is that CFL's are not compatible with dimmer switches. For residential use, look for color-corrected bulbs that emit a softer light.

HALOGEN

Superior light and outstanding color quality of halogen bulbs make them an excellent choice for kitchens. The clean, white light emitted from these bulbs closely resembles natural daylight, and reduces eye strain when reading or working in the kitchen. Halogen bulbs burn brighter, longer and consume less energy than incandescent bulbs. However, because halogen burns so intensely, this type of bulb is better suited for task or recessed lighting, or fixtures where the light is shielded from the eye. Another option is to place halogen lights on dimmers to reduce the intensity when it is not needed. The price of a halogen bulb is roughly four to five time that of an incandescent bulb.

XENON

One of the latest style of bulb on the market, Xenon bulbs were developed for commercial use but are steadily making their way to the home market. Offered as an improved version of the halogen bulb, Xenon bulbs burn cooler and last nearly twice as long. An added benefit is that Xenon bulbs do not emit UV-rays that can fade fabrics and some materials over time. Not surprisingly, the cost of a Xenon bulb is double that of halogen.

Opposite page, top Glass pendants suspended on fabric-covered cords are well placed to provide ambient and task lighting.

PROGRAMMABLE LIGHTS

▶ MAKE THE MOST OF A MULTI-LAYERED LIGHTING PLAN BY ADDING A PROGRAMMABLE CONTROL SYSTEM THAT ADJUSTS LIGHTING TO MATCH THE MOOD AND FUNCTION OF THE ROOM.

▶ FOR EXAMPLE, A FOOD PREPARATION SETTING FULLY ILLUMINATES TASK AND OVERHEAD LIGHTS FOR SETTING THE TABLE AND COOKING THE MEAL. WHEN GUESTS ARRIVE, YOU CAN SWITCH TO AN ENTERTAINING MODE THAT SIMULTANEOUSLY TURNS OFF OVERHEAD LIGHTING, DIMS TASK LIGHTS, BRINGS UP ACCENT LIGHTING, AND EVEN TURNS ON FAVORITE DINNER MUSIC.

▶ THE SYSTEM HAS A SAFETY AND SECURITY SETTING THAT TURNS ON SPECIFIC OUTDOOR LIGHTS AT DUSK, OR TURNS ON LIGHTS THAT LEAD THE WAY INTO THE KITCHEN WHEN YOU ARRIVE HOME AFTER DARK.

▶ CONTROLS ARE AVAILABLE IN EITHER WALL MOUNTED PANELS OR AS HAND-HELD REMOTE UNITS.

Middle left Task lights beneath upper cabinets illuminate countertop surfaces, and a fitting in the hood lights the cooktop below and brings the backsplash into focus.

Bottom left Bright lights hanging over the countertop provide excellent task lighting. Natural light is good in this vast airy kitchen, too.

A P P L I A N C E S

The best way to select appliances is to match the way you use it with the design and performance of the item in question. Here, you will find information about the range, the cooktop and oven, the microwave, the dishwasher, refrigeration and ventilation.

Right

In a kitchen with such interesting cabinetry design appliances can be hidden from view behind the cabinet doors.

THE RANGE

A range consolidates cooking functions by combining the cooktop, one or more ovens, and the broiler in one appliance. Contrasted with a kitchen configuration that features, for example, a separate cooktop, wall oven, and freestanding microwave, the range offers space-saving efficiency. Ranges are fuelled either by gas or electric heat, and fall into three categories: Freestanding, slide-in, or drop-in units.

▶ Freestanding units are the conventional choice. They sit directly on the floor and are the easiest to install.

▶ Slide-in ranges have unfinished sides because they are permanently installed between two base cabinets.

▶ Drop-in ranges fit into a counter or island and are supported by a base cabinet.

Whether or not you choose a range that is powered by gas or electric could depend upon the location of your home; gas is unavailable in certain areas, and costly to install in homes that are not already hooked up to the utility. That said, many seasoned chefs prefer cooking with gas because it offers rapid heating as well as the ability to modulate the flame to accommodate different styles of cooking. On the other hand, gas ranges have more parts, can be difficult to clean and generally require more maintenance than electric appliances.

In what are known as 'heat and serve' households, where cooking is reserved for holidays and special occasions, a smooth-top, electric range with a self-cleaning oven, and built-in microwave might be a more practical choice.

For bakers, electric ovens offer an even heat and can produce better results with baking than gas appliances. Dual-fuel ranges that feature gas cooktops with electric ovens are another option to consider.

Once you have determined the range style and heat source you prefer, narrow your choices by checking each appliance to see it has the features you require. Compare each manufacturer's top- of-the-line offering to see which of the many features, such as you will actually use on a regular basis. In many cases, the basic cooking function is the same but the higher cost reflects expensive add-ons such as sophisticated timers, touch controls and special finishes. Once you have eliminated the features that do not fit your needs, compare warranties and energy efficiency labels on the remaining appliances. Keep in mind that gathering information on appliance styles and features and taking the time to evaluate your cooking, dining, and entertaining patterns will help you make an informed decision that will steer you to the most suitable range.

Above The range shown here has a cover for the cooking top, creating an extra work surface when you are baking or roasting.

THE COOKTOP

A separate cooktop enables two cooks to function efficiently-while one prepares vegetables and sauces at the stove, another can be baking or broiling at a wall-mounted oven in another part of the room. However, this configuration requires more space dedicated to appliances and may cost more because of the additional hookups required for multiple units.

The most important feature of the cooktop is the burner configuration. Most models have between four to six elements of differing sizes to accommodate an assortment of cookware. The basic electric cooktops offer conventional coil elements, whereas ceramic glass smooth tops with quick-heating quartz halogen burners are a feature of the most expensive cooktops.

Gas ranges use metal grids to suspend cookware over the flame. Choose a model with sturdy, smooth grids that enable you to slide, rather than lift, heavy pots on and off burners. Also consider sealed gas burners that contain spills and are easy to clean. Other special features you can expect to find on both gas and electric cooktops include warming zones to hold prepared dishes until the entire meal is ready to serve, and convenient bridge burners that work by converting two small burners into one large element suitable for oversized cookware or roasting pans.

Right On this cooktop, heavy-duty burner grates accommodate oversized cookware and provide a smooth surface for sliding, rather than lifting, heavy pots and pan from front to back burners.

SUIT YOURSELF

▶ FOR COOKS WHO HAVE GROWN ACCUSTOMED TO USING A PARTICULAR STYLE OF COOKWARE, FINDING THE RIGHT FIT FOR FAVORITE POTS AND PANS IS ANOTHER CONSIDERATION WHEN SELECTING APPLIANCES. ENSURE THAT COOKTOP BURNER CONFIGURATIONS ARE AMPLE ENOUGH TO ACCOMMODATE YOUR LARGEST PIECES WITHOUT BLOCKING ADJACENT ELEMENTS. ON SOME APPLIANCES, BURNERS ARE PLACED SO CLOSE TOGETHER THAT LARGE PIECES OF COOKWARE ONLY FIT ON FRONT BURNERS, MAKING IT DIFFICULT TO COOK MORE THAN ONE OR TWO DISHES AT A TIME. ALSO KEEP IN MIND THAT CERTAIN TYPES OF APPLIANCES REQUIRE SPECIAL COOKWARE. SOME SMOOTH-TOP ELECTRIC RANGES AND COOKTOPS CALL FOR SPECIAL FLAT-BOTTOMED POTS AND PANS.

▶ IF YOU ARE PLANNING ON PURCHASING A COMMERCIAL RANGE, ALSO PLAN FOR A SET OF COMMERCIAL-QUALITY COOKWARE TO GO WITH IT. THE INTENSE HEAT OF THE GAS BURNERS IS TOO MUCH FOR COOKWARE DESIGNED FOR RESIDENTIAL USE.

THE OVEN

The first thing to check when comparing ovens is capacity. Though individual ovens may appear to be the same size on the outside, interior cavities may dramatically differ in size due to rack configuration, light and fan placement, and insulation. When measuring oven capacity, measure from the lowest rack to the top heating element to get an accurate picture of what will fit inside.

Electric ovens often produce better results than gas-fired ovens because they offer more even heating and fewer "hot spots." Conventional electric ovens have two elements; one located on the bottom of the oven for baking and roasting foods, and one located on the top of the interior cavity for broiling. If you do a great deal of baking, consider buying a convection oven—an oven equipped with fans that continuously circulate heat throughout the cavity,

Above

A stainless steel double wall oven unit expands cooking options by pairing a conventional oven for roasting and broiling, with an oven for baking on the bottom.

SPEED-COOKING OVENS

▶ THESE OVENS COMBINE THE BEST OF MICROWAVE AND CONVENTIONAL OVEN TECHNOLOGY TO COOK FOOD FASTER WITHOUT COMPROMISING FLAVOR. THEY USE MICROWAVE ENERGY TO RAPIDLY COOK THE INSIDE OF FOOD, WHILE CONVENTIONAL HEAT CIRCULATES TO SEAL IN MOISTURE AND ROAST, BROWN, OR BROIL THE FOOD SURFACE. COOKING TIMES ARE REDUCED BY AS MUCH AS 75%. PRICED SLIGHTLY HIGHER THAN CONVENTIONAL OVENS, LOOK FOR MODELS WITH TOUCH PAD CONTROLS THAT OFFER PRE-PROGRAMMED COOKING TIMES FOR MORE COMMONLY PREPARED FOODS SUCH AS ROAST CHICKEN OR BAKED POTATOES.

minimizing hot and cold spots. As a result, food cooks faster at lower temperatures. However, the circulated air can cause some foods, especially meats, to dry out quickly. In addition, if you have never used a convection oven, you will have to adjust baking times when using recipes that were written for conventional ovens.

If your appliance configuration calls for a double wall oven, consider buying models that offer both conventional and convection heating. In kitchens with just one oven, consider appliances that offer the option of switching back and forth between conventional and convection modes to get the best results for all types of foods.

THE MICROWAVE

Microwaves are available in three styles: Freestanding units, built-in models, and over-the-range microwaves that replace the vent hood by integrating an exhaust fan and work light. There is also a range of combination microwave/convection ovens that can brown, bake, or roast, unlike a regular microwave.

In most households, the primary function of the microwave is defrosting, reheating, or snack preparation, as opposed to actual cooking. Because of this, it makes sense to locate the appliance outside of the basic work triangle when possible.

Consider installing the microwave level with a workspace or countertop to create a snack area or landing spot for heated foods as they come out of the oven. Also consider its capacity before you buy. If the microwave use will be limited to heating individual serving bowls and dinner plates, buying a larger model may simply take up valuable space in the kitchen.

On the other hand, if you use the microwave for preparing large quantities of food, or several dishes at a time, consider investing in a model that features removable racks, multiple cooking sensors, and pre-programmed settings for a variety of foods.

On a practical note, think about door clearance when placing the microwave. Since the majority of models are hinged on the left, make sure your kitchen design includes ample room for it to open and that you can gain full access to the interior.

Right   A range topped with a microwave integrates cooking functions into one convenient location.

Far right, top   Installed above the range this microwave oven includes a built-in exhaust fan as well as task lighting for cooking.

Bottom   When counter space is at a premium, build a recessed niche in the cabinetry for the microwave.

REFRIGERATION

Evaluate your household's cooking and shopping patterns to determine the style and capacity of refrigeration best suited to your requirements. This is important. For instance, if you have a big family, prefer to shop just once a week, and cook or freeze large quantities of food, consider buying a large refrigerator with a spacious freezer, adjustable shelves, and different temperature zones for storing a variety of foods. That way, you have a refrigerator that suits the way you live.

For households with fewer people, those who regularly dine out, or visit the market several times a week, consider buying a smaller appliance with fewer features would be a more practical and economical choice.

There are two basic categories of refrigerators; freestanding and built-in. Freestanding units are larger and less expensive but are generally deeper than standard kitchen cabinets, meaning they may jut out into the room. Built-in units are smaller, shallower and fit flush with cabinets. Many offer custom-matched panels which make the appliance virtually disappear into its surroundings. Not surprisingly, built-in refrigerators are also more costly.

The interior of the refrigerator is measured in cubic feet. Though many shoppers assume that more cubic feet equals extra storage space, that is not always the case. A better way to evaluate refrigerators is to compare interior storage. Some smaller units may be designed so efficiently that they may offer more space than larger, bulkier units. Look for adaptable shelves that easily shift to accommodate different-sized containers, deep compartments on doors, and clear vegetable bins that allow you to view contents without opening the drawers.

Water and ice dispensers add convenience, but they can take up as much as twenty-five percent of freezer storage. Also, since the refrigerator uses more electricity than any other kitchen appliance, energy efficiency makes another basis for comparison. The EnergyGuide Label, required by law to appear on major appliances, provides an estimate of the units of electricity and cost required to run the appliance per year.

Refrigerators are designed in three styles: Side-by-side, freezer on top, and freezer on bottom. Side-by-side units offer easy access to refrigeration and freezer compartments without bending. Also, since the doors do not swing as wide as the other models, they make a good choice for smaller spaces. On the other hand, neither compartment is as spacious as those found on single door units, making it difficult to store large trays and platters. Single door models with the freezer either on the top or bottom offer better space distribution and better accommodate different sized containers. Freezer-on-top models outsell all others, but before you buy consider that the refrigerator door is opened far more than the freezer. Buying a unit with the freezer on the bottom means less bending and better visibility of the foods you use most.

Left Capped with custom cabinetry, a large capacity refrigerator features smooth door panels that integrate the unit with the rest of the kitchen.

THE WINE CHILLER

► THE WINE REFRIGERATOR IS A LITTLE
TOUCH OF LUXURY EASILY INCORPORATED
INTO JUST ABOUT ANY KITCHEN. MOST
UNITS ARE NO LARGER THAN A DISHWASHER
AND ARE DESIGNED TO FIT BENEATH THE
KITCHEN COUNTER, INTO A BUTLER'S
PANTRY, OR ANYWHERE THAT YOU
ENTERTAIN. LOOK FOR MODELS THAT
FEATURE TWO OR THREE TEMPERATURE
ZONES TO MAINTAIN THE IDEAL CLIMATE AND
HUMIDITY LEVEL FOR A VARIETY OF WINES

► RACKS SHOULD BE ADJUSTABLE, AND
"CANTED," OR SLIGHTLY TILTED. IF YOU
SELECT A WINE REFRIGERATOR WITH GLASS
DOORS, ENSURE THAT THEY ARE TINTED
AND TEMPERED TO FILTER DAMAGING RAYS
AND PRESERVE THE WINE'S FLAVOR.

► OTHER OPTIONS WORTH CONSIDERING
INCLUDE INTERIOR LIGHTING, DOOR LOCKS,
AND CUSTOM DOOR PANELS DESIGNED TO
BLEND WITH THE SURROUNDING CABINETRY.

DISHWASHER

First introduced as a luxury item for 1950's
era housewives, the dishwasher has become
a modern day necessity for time-pressed
people and especially for busy families.

In fact, it has become increasingly
common for many homeowners to
incorporate not one, but two dishwashers,
into new kitchen designs. Think of the
dishwasher as the kitchen workhorse. Over
the course of a week, the dishwasher will
often see more use than any other appliance
in the kitchen-with the exception of the
refrigerator. When doing your research for a
dishwasher, you will find a wide range of
features and prices. While it is true that even

Below A custom
dishwasher panel
makes the
appliance
practically
disappear when the
door is closed.
A concealed
control panel
contributes to the
streamlined styling.

THE DISHWASHING DRAWER

▶ THESE SMALL-CAPACITY UNITS ARE SIZED FOR KITCHENS THAT DO NOT HAVE ROOM FOR A FULL-SIZE APPLIANCE, OR THEY CAN USED AS A SECOND DISHWASHER TO ASSIST WITH CLEANING UP AFTER AN EVENT IN ANOTHER PART OF THE ROOM.

▶ DISHWASHING DRAWERS ARE DESIGNED TO SLIDE INTO A 24" (60CM) SPACE AND HOLD UP TO 12 AVERAGE-SIZE DINNER PLATES.

▶ WHEN INSTALLED IN A BUTLER'S PANTRY, A DISHWASHING DRAWER ENABLES GLASSWARE AND CRYSTAL TO BE WASHED WITHIN CLOSE PROXIMITY OF THE DINING TABLE AND STORAGE CABINETS.

▶ IN SMALL, APARTMENT-SIZED KITCHENS REPLACING A CABINET WITH ONE OF THESE DRAWERS ADDS CONVENIENCE WITHOUT THE SACRIFICE OF MUCH STORAGE SPACE.

▶ CHOOSE ONE DRAWER FOR SMALL SPACES, OR MAYBE STACK TWO AS AN ENERGY-EFFICIENT ALTERNATIVE THAT USES LESS WATER AND ELECTRICITY THAN A REGULAR DISHWASHER. LOOK FOR MODELS THAT OFFER AT LEAST THREE WASH CYCLES, AND ARE QUIET WHEN IN OPERATION.

the most basic models perform the dishwashing task well, higher-priced dishwashers offer better quality construction and many sophisticated technical features.

The biggest advance in dishwashers over the last decade has been that of noise reduction. The droning hum of the dishwasher has been replaced with "whisper-quiet" operation achieved with the inclusion of better insulation and low-noise motors in the product. Not surprisingly, the quieter the dishwasher, the higher the price.

Other features to look for include dishwashers with built-in food disposal units and pot-scrubbing features that eliminate rinsing and scraping. Stainless steel wash tubs, increasingly available on lower end models, are more durable than plastic, promote better energy efficiency, and allow the unit to operate at higher temperatures for sanitizing dishes.

Also compare rack options. More flexibility in loading means a wider range of uses in the kitchen. The rack systems on some dishwashers have been reconfigured to make way for roasting pans, stockpots, and even high chair trays.

At the most expensive end of the spectrum, you will find sleek, European-manufactured dishwashers that boast of high energy efficiency, a compact design, super quiet performance, water-filtering systems, plus a realm of sophisticated sensors that make the dishwasher run with race-car precision. For about one third of the price, expect a basic model that will get the job done, be reasonably quiet, but offer fewer features and rack configurations.

VENTILATION

In kitchens layouts where a large stove hood would obstruct sight lines, or pose a logistics problem, an alternative is to install a downdraft system that whisks air down into vents located on or behind the cooking surface. However, the downdraft system, though adequate, is not as effective as an overhead hood in pulling steam and particles from the air, and would not be considered powerful enough to vent a commercial-style range or cooktop.

The placement of your cooking appliance is another consideration when selecting a ventilation system. Installing a range in an alcove, or surrounding it on either side with cabinets creates a barrier that efficiently directs heat and steam into the ventilation system. Cooktops or ranges that are out in the open, or set into islands, are more affected by cross-currents from other parts of the room, making it more difficult to capture air before it escapes. In these cases, lowering the hood or adding a more powerful exhaust fan will usually solve the problem.

Features to look for in a ventilation system include:

▶ Quiet operation. Some fans generate a small amount of noise while others bring conversation to a standstill.

▶ Air filters. Inspect filters to make sure that they are easy to remove and clean.

▶ Task lighting. In overhead hoods, look for lighting that shines directly onto the cooking surface.

Left An architectural cover with elegant wood trim makes a striking statement that blends with the overall style of the kitchen.

The kitchen's ventilation system removes much of the heat, grease, and moisture that accumulate during cooking. Here, the key is to install a system powerful enough to keep the kitchen clean and comfortable by venting steam and cooking odors to the outside. Since heat rises, the most efficient form of ventilation is a range hood installed directly over the cooking source. To maximize efficiency, the hood should measure as deep as the range or cooktop, and extend out at least three inches (7.5cm) on either side.

Though many homeowners like the sleek look of exposed stainless steel or copper hoods, some prefer to conceal the hood behind elaborate tile or carved wood facades that better reflect the kitchen's unique design scheme.

THE SINK

Merging form with function is the
ultimate in design, and contemporary
sinks have been engineered to include
both of these design elements. New
materials plumb new depths of
durability, while familiar and unusual
shapes endear themselves to us. This
chapter looks at sinks, faucets,
backsplashes and waste disposal
units to add to your dream list.

Right A double sink
with deep bowls forged in
stainless steel strikes the
perfect balance in a
kitchen designed for
entertaining.

Pâtes
BARONI

THE KITCHEN SINK

Since most cooking and cleaning tasks require water, the sink is often the busiest spot in the kitchen. Accordingly, it makes sense to buy the largest sink that suits your design and your selected cabinet can accommodate.

If you have enough space to add a second sink elsewhere in the kitchen, it will help to cut down on foot traffic in the work triangle. When selecting the primary sink, keep in mind that it should be wide enough to soak a large roasting pan. Depth is also important. Look for a sink that is deep enough for both washing dishes and cleaning vegetables, but not so deep that it requires you bend down to reach the bottom. If you prefer a split sink, select an extra-wide model with an oversized bowl on one side, and a smaller bowl on the other. This arrangement enables more tasks than double sinks split down the middle.

Sink location is everything. Positioning the water source close to workspaces and the range cuts down on the number of steps it takes to complete cooking tasks. In fact, most designers begin the kitchen plan by placing the sink in the most advantageous spot and arranging the other features around it. If space permits, it is best to place the sink at the center of the cabinet, and surround it on both sides by wide drain boards, with one side devoted to food preparation, and the other side to cleaning up.

Once you have selected the type of sink to fit your needs, match it with the other materials and also ensure that it suits the style of the design. Here is a brief description of the most popular options for sinks:

STAINLESS STEEL

Durable and versatile, stainless steel sinks account for more than half of all kitchen sinks sold in the US. Stainless sinks offer easy care and a timeless look that transcends trends. Though you can expect to find a broad range of styles and sizes, it pays to purchase the best quality you can afford. Stainless steel is sold in gauges that refer to the thickness of the steel. A lower gauge means thicker steel, or better quality. An 18-gauge sink is considered top residential quality. Another aspect to consider is the sink's sound- muffling ability. Since stainless tends to be noisy, look for sinks that have a sound- deadening undercoating. Finally, satin or brushed finishes will conceal scratches, require lower maintenance and generally look better longer than stainless sinks with mirror finishes.

COPPER

Copper sinks add warm metallic tones to a kitchen. A hard-wearing metal, it holds up beautifully with proper care. Because it oxidizes when exposed to air, regular polishing is necessary to maintain the finish. Hammered copper camouflages scratches and is generally a better choice than a smooth-surface bowl. Because of cost and

Above The unique shape and beautiful texture of a small copper sink adds warm metallic tone that richly accents a marble-topped island.

▶ **UNDERMOUNT:** SINK BOWL IS ATTACHED BENEATH THE COUNTERTOP WITH NO VISIBLE RIM.

▶ **RIMMED:** COMMON ON STAINLESS STEEL SINKS; A FLAT METAL RIM SURROUNDS THE SINK, CONNECTING THE BOWL TO THE COUNTERTOP.

▶ **SELF-RIMMING:** THE SINK BOWL IS SURROUNDED BY A LIP THAT FORMS A SEAL WHEN DROPPED INTO THE CABINET OPENING.

▶ **INTEGRAL:** SINK AND COUNTERTOP ARE MANUFACTURED AND INSTALLED AS ONE PIECE.

▶ **TILE-IN:** A STYLE OF SINK DESIGNED TO MOUNT FLUSH AGAINST TILED COUNTERTOPS

Above left The food preparation area around this slim sink is clad in Dura limestone.

Above right The bar sink takes on a new look when cast in a stunning copper finish. The undermount sink is attached beneath countertops that extend over its rim.

maintenance, some people choose copper for an island or second sink.

CAST-IRON

Porcelain-coated cast iron evokes a distinctive farmhouse style. Though the cast-iron base is nearly indestructible, the porcelain coating can chip if heavy pots and pans are accidentally dropped into the sink. The surface is also less forgiving when it comes to glassware and fine crystal, and care is advised when washing these items. Though the porcelain top coat is prone to staining, a non-abrasive cleanser can usually restore the surface. Modern sinks are available in a wide range of color and styles.

SOLID SURFACE

Many homeowners prefer the smooth transition between countertop and sink that solid-surface sinks offer. Molded into the surrounding countertop with no visible ridges or lines, solid-surface sinks get high marks for both form and function. Custom-made to your specification, these sinks are manufactured in colors and styles to blend with your décor. Though solid surface is easy to maintain, scratches and dents that appear with wear may require professional sanding. Also, they are among the most expensive models of sinks on the market.

COMPOSITE

Made of natural stone bonded with an acrylic material, composite sinks are durable, and are available in a wide range of colors and configurations. While they feature the beauty of natural stone, acrylic polymers make composite sinks heat and scratch resistant. Uniform color that goes all the way through the sink means any flaws are barely discernable, even if the sink is chipped or dented. This type of sink is available from the cheaper, basic designs to expensive top of the line models that feature integrated sprays, soap dispensers, and built-in dish racks.

FAUCETS

The faucet has come into its own as a design-led kitchen fitting, and now has a wide range of functions.

The type of faucet you select may be determined by the style of sink chosen, particularly if you have selected a sink with pre-drilled holes. (Faucets require one, two, or three holes for installation.) Those installed in a single opening may come with separate handles mounted on the spout for hot and cold water, or a single handle. Single-handed units are a good option for the kitchen because they can easily be operated when you are holding a pot in one hand and have the other free.

Generally speaking the design rule is to match the faucet finish to that of the cabinet hardware, or choose a style that reflects the overall décor of the kitchen. Though faucets come in a range of decorative finishes, the underlying base metal is nearly always brass, which is unaffected by prolonged exposure to water. Popular faucet finishes include nickel, antique brass, gold-plate, polished and brushed chrome, colored epoxy, and "split-finishes," which combine two or more metals.

While faucet finish may set the style of the kitchen, the shape and features of the fitting dictate the function. If the sink is shallow, consider a tall curved faucet for filling large pots. For wide, double sinks, the faucet should swivel far enough to reach both bowls. Also be sure that the faucet extends to the middle of the sink bowl, and not merely to the edge. If your sink deck does not include room for a sprayer, look for faucets that integrate the sprayer into the unit.

Purchasing the sink and faucet at the same time enables you to find the most suitable combination of style and function for your kitchen. Also consider other features that you may want to add such as a separate hot water tap, a soap dispenser, or a water filtration system, and make sure that there is adequate space to include them. If your faucet is deck mounted, meaning that it will be installed on the counter behind the sink, be sure to personally place the fittings yourself before the contractor drills holes in the surface.

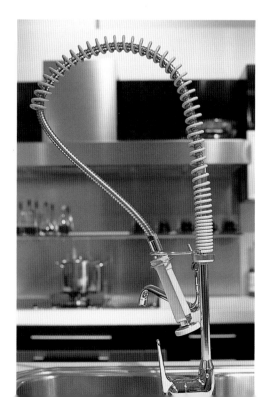

Top A classic faucet with a mixer.

Left A flexible spray attachment streamlines tasks and swings wide enough to reach both sides of a large double sink.

THE POT-FILLER FAUCET

▶ THE POT-FILLER FAUCET, ONCE CONSIDERED A COMMERCIAL KITCHEN FEATURE, HAS BEEN MAKING ITS WAY TO THE MAINSTREAM OF RESIDENTIAL DESIGN OVER THE LAST FEW YEARS. INSTALLED BEHIND THE STOVE, THIS SPECIAL FAUCET ALLOWS THE COOK TO FILL LARGE STOCKPOTS WITH WATER DIRECTLY ON THE HEAT SOURCE, WITHOUT HAVING TO TRANSPORT FROM THE SINK. IF YOU FREQUENTLY COOK LARGE QUANTITIES OF PASTA, SOUPS, OR STOCKS, AND IF YOUR RANGE IS POSITIONED SO IT CAN ACCOMMODATE THE EXTRA PLUMBING LINE, ADDING A POT-FILLER FAUCET MAY BE A HANDY OPTION. HOWEVER, LIKE ANY PLUMBING OR ELECTRICAL FEATURE, KEEP IN MIND THAT ADDING THIS FEATURE TO A NEW KITCHEN IS FAR EASIER AND LESS EXPENSIVE THAN TO A REMODELED SPACE. ONE MORE THING TO THINK ABOUT: ALTHOUGH IT IS TRUE THAT FILLING THE COOKING VESSEL ON TOP OF THE RANGE SAVES HEAVY LIFTING, LARGE POTS OF COOKED PASTA STILL HAVE TO BE DRAINED. A DESIGN ALTERNATIVE MIGHT BE TO INCLUDE A SECOND SINK WITHIN A FEW STEPS OF THE RANGE FOR FILLING, AND DRAINING, HEAVY POTS.

Left Installed above the cooktop is a convenient pot-filler faucet that eliminates the need to lift heavy stockpots. They can be filled directly at the heat source.

Above Single-lever faucets offer easy, hands-free operation for cooks with limited mobility.

BACKSPLASHES

Whether you choose bold color, elegant pattern or subdued tone and texture, use the backsplash to create a design to complement the kitchen.

Though its basic function is to protect walls from cooking spills and splashes, the backsplash—located vertically between countertops and cabinets—has evolved into an important location to add a design style statement in the kitchen. Whatever surface you choose for this space, there are a few design aspects to consider.

Selecting backsplash materials in the same color and texture as surrounding cabinetry works to unify the kitchen décor. Conversely, selecting a contrasting color or material for the backsplash establishes a focal point.

Here again, choices abound. You can choose to use hand-painted tiles to design an elegant mosaic in the European style; add subtle texture with a glass or a crumpled metal tile design, or simply repeat the same material you selected for use on countertops to give the backsplash a sleek look.

Care is another consideration. Though the backsplash will take less of a beating than kitchen countertops, choosing a low-maintenance material that can be wiped down with cleaning fluid and water will keep these surfaces sparkling. A stainless steel backsplash, the chef's choice, looks modern and effective, and is easy to clean.

Above Lattice-pattern ceramic tile, edged with a raised border, creates an appealing bas-relief inset that stands out against an all-white backsplash.

Below Tumbled stone, set on a diagonal and framed with a contrasting tile border, makes an easy-to-clean, smooth backsplash.

WASTE DISPOSAL

Little things can make a big difference in the kitchen. Take the garbage disposal. Once installed, it is quite likely that the next time you will have to think about it is when it needs to be repaired or replaced. Waste disposal, while perhaps not as interesting as say, selecting tile or choosing appliances, nonetheless plays a strong, supporting role in the day to day function of the kitchen. Best of all, setting up kitchen waste systems from the start carves out the space to integrate them into the overall design, making them less obtrusive.

Before you buy a garbage disposal for your kitchen, check local codes to see if the appliance is permitted in your area. In some parts of the country, their use is regulated and installation may require a special permit or inspection. In the overall scheme of things, selecting a disposal is fairly straightforward. Large capacity models with stainless steel components have the best repair record and will last the longest. Though there are plenty of inexpensive disposals available at home centers, the motors on lower quality models tend to backup easier and wear out faster. Since the price difference between a basic disposal and a top of the line model is as little as a hundred dollars, it pays to purchase a reputable brand with a good warranty to eliminate headaches and plumbing problems down the road.

Elsewhere in the kitchen, locate trash bins in base cabinets close to where food preparation and cleaning up tasks take place. In large kitchens, consider placing one bin next to the sink and another in the island. Most cabinet manufacturers offer built-in accessories that slide out when the cabinet door is open; and back in when the door closes. Some offer a hands-free option similar to a step-on can where a pedal, installed on the floor beneath the cabinet, pops the door open giving access when your hands are full.

Since glass, metal, paper, and plastics are now sorted for collection in most parts of the country, designers are incorporating recycling centers into new kitchens. And, while this feature saves time and adds convenience, the major drawback is the amount of cabinet space required; space that might otherwise be devoted to storage.

If you like the idea of organizing recycling close to kitchen task areas, one solution is to set up a center in a nearby laundry or utility room. The most efficient systems are those that collect materials in bins that can be taken out to the curb for collection. Consider adapting a base cabinet with recycling bins that slide or tilt out for easy removal.

In homes where the utility or laundry room is situated next to the garage, you might be able to set up a two-way recycling center that opens on both sides of the cabinet.

Right A trash bin tucked into a base cabinet provides a convenient place to clean up close to the food preparation area.The mechanism adjusts to accommodate several sizes of waste cans.

PART TWO

CASE STUDIES

CALIFORNIA

With the major design elements already in place, cherry cabinets and sophisticated surfaces were used to redefine a rustic California kitchen and frame its finest feature.

Remodeling projects come in all shapes in sizes. Some kitchens require such extensive modification that the real challenge is figuring out where to begin. Others, like this San Francisco kitchen, are so well made that even after a few decades, all that is required is a bit of freshening up.

The kitchen is situated in a hilltop home perched at the top of a wide valley that offers breathtaking mountain views, golden sunsets, and front row seats to watch the fog roll in from the ocean.

The large, L-shape floor plan had ample room for cooking and dining with enough space left over for a convenient desk, and a walk-in pantry. The materials palette, rust-colored brick set against neutral wood tones, was already warm and appealing.

Right Granite countertops and cherry wood cabinetry shifted the tone from rustic to refined.

DREAMING

Above The kitchen's pine cathedral ceiling soars to a dramatic height.

Opposite page An inset granite backsplash behind the range adds elegant character to the kitchen.

<table>
<tr><td colspan="2">DESIGN SUMMARY</td></tr>
</table>

DESIGN SUMMARY

- Tongue-and-groove pine ceiling
- Cherry cabinetry
- Red oak flooring
- Polished granite surfaces
- Copper accents

Then, there was the tongue-and-groove pine ceiling that spectacularly soars 16ft (6.5m) above the floor, forming the kitchen's primary focal point. With the kitchen's good bones as his framework, designer Albert Carey simply retooled the original rustic tone of the space to reflect a more refined, sophisticated look that gave the twenty-five-year-old room a fresh feel.

The kitchen's original oak cabinets, one of the room's most prominent design elements, were past their prime and imparted a country kitchen character that did not to justice to the home's Mediterranean-style architecture. Expansive tile countertops were difficult to clean, and row upon row of square grout lines formed a monotonous design element that distracted from the kitchen's more attractive features.

The first phase of the facelift was replacing the oak cabinets. New, custom cherry wood cabinets instantly updated the look and softly accented the room's brickwork and red oak flooring. In addition, the understated texture and tight grain of the cherry wood balanced the pine and allowed

Right New custom cabinetry with beadboard door panels complements the kitchen's existing red oak flooring.

Above Adding an outlet to the inside of a small corner of the hutch made it possible to conceal a 'kitchen-sized' flat panel screen behind a lift-up panel.

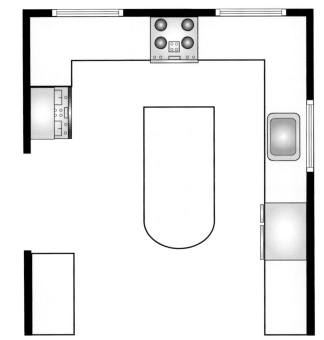

the tall ceiling to take center stage in the room. Detailed with recessed panel doors, beadboard trim, and antique pewter handles and pulls, the new cabinets add sophistication without diminishing the casual feel of the space.

Next, two different types of granite were selected to replace ceramic tile surfaces. Though the stone used on perimeter counters is remarkably similar to that used on the island, a slight variation in color adds subtle texture that visually delineates the expansive surfaces. Carey's clever design concept is best illustrated behind the range where inset stone creates a beautiful backsplash beneath a gleaming copper range hood.

At the core of the kitchen space is a well-planned chef's kitchen where traditionally prepared dishes are at the heart of family gatherings and cultural celebrations. New appliances that include a dual fuel, six-burner gas range, convection wall oven and commercial refrigeration support her cooking style and greatly improve the function of the revamped kitchen. While the spacious kitchen comfortably seats up to 12 for casual dinners, more formal meals are served in the dining room connected to the kitchen by way of a graceful brick archway.

Squaring off one end of the center island made a wide workspace close to the range and oven area, while rounding off the other side created a seating area where guests gather to socialize as the meal is prepared. A detailed, ogee edge softens the

Above The kitchen's roomy L-shaped layout includes a generous island, a sit-down dining area, and a desk.

appearance of the vast granite surface which is among the largest slabs Carey has installed. Above the island, a sculpted wrought-iron pot rack anchored to the ceiling integrates convenient storage for copper cookware as well as task lighting that shines down on the surface below.

At the bottom of the L-shape layout, a glass-enclosed dining atrium and desk looks out over the treetops. A retractable awning was added to shade the room from the afternoon sun, making the desk area the homeowner's favorite place to make phone calls or catch up on paperwork. Across from the dining area, a built-in hutch configured from kitchen cabinets has display space for artwork, storage for glasses and dinnerware, and a space for a flat-panel television that is easily viewed from the table and desk.

Top A deep, brushed-stainless sink and tall goose neck faucet with sprayer attachment makes it easy to fill and soak large cookware and roasting pans. An air switch behind the sink operates the garbage disposal.

Above left The backsplash behind the cooking range.

Above right The home's original red-oak floors retained their smooth texture even after 25 years of wear in the high-traffic kitchen.

Above A wrought iron pot rack suspended over the center island adds architectural interest and places copper cookware within easy reach of the sink and range. The 6 ft (2 m) tall rack was installed in the cathedral ceiling.

Left Wrought-iron and wood chairs are placed at the rounded end of the island where many of the informal meals are eaten.

MELLOW CHERRY

The redesign of a confined kitchen yields a gracious gathering space filled with the family's favourite features.

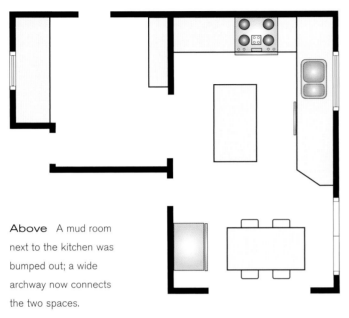

Above A mud room next to the kitchen was bumped out; a wide archway now connects the two spaces.

Left A masterful mix of cherry wood, painted cabinets, and architectural detail characterize the new kitchen/dining area.

Above right
The casual dining table and chairs are close to the island and food serving area.

When it comes to design inspiration, anything can serve as a starting point; in the case of this kitchen, it was a defective cooktop. When the couple began working with kitchen design company, Design Consultants, they were simply looking to upgrade their outdated range with a commercial appliance that suited the husband's gourmet cooking style.

However, as is often the case when it comes to home improvement projects, a search for a single appliance evolved into a large-scale remodel that reconfigured the home's central living space. The "before" floor plan lacked character and cohesiveness. Plus, a choppy layout meant that family members were relegated to separate areas of the home to perform routine household tasks.

The assignment began with an evaluation of the family's lifestyle. The two-career couple and their young son treasure the time they spend together. They entertain frequently and desired a casual, yet elegant space that would support a broad range of family activities.

- Stained cherry and painted wood cabinets
- Polished granite surfaces
- Tumbled stone accents
- Timber floor
- Lighting task and hidden lights

While an epicurean kitchen figured prominently in the husband's vision, his wife's wish-list included relocating the washer and dryer from the basement to a convenient laundry on the main level. Modifying the existing U-shaped kitchen meant manipulating the space within the existing perimeters to maximize its efficiency. To set the plan in motion, an existing long peninsula that confined movement in the kitchen was replaced with an island made of cherry wood that dramatically improved the function and feel of the room.

Next, a six-burner commercial cook top was placed against the kitchen's exterior wall to vent heat and steam to the outside of the home. A gleaming stainless backsplash, ventilation hood, and a handy pot filler faucet fulfilled the husband's wish of a professional, quality, cooking zone in the kitchen. For added convenience, a spacious warming drawer beneath the cook top accommodates the family's staggered eating schedules by keeping dinner warm for the late arrivals.

To create cabinet storage, the design plan called for moving the oven and microwave to the center island. Along with freeing up valuable wall space, lowering the microwave makes it possible for the son to

Top A built-in hutch was configured from cabinet components and customized with a mosaic tile pattern and subtle accent lighting.

Above, left The pot-filler's handle is fashioned from a reclaimed radiator handle.

Above, right Honey oak flooring was a natural choice for creating warm character and texture.

prepare his own snacks. Steps away from the island, a large table with comfortable chairs anchors a casual dining area used for everyday meals.

A curved arch leads to a luxury laundry area, created by bumping out a small mud room next to the kitchen. As well as opening up the two areas, the archway lets natural light into the kitchen. The laundry's elegant touches, including custom cherry wood cabinetry to conceal appliances, and a granite folding table, elevate a hum-drum task to the height of style and efficiency.

Once the three main function areas were mapped out, materials were the key to linking them visually. Repeated use of traditional cherry cabinetry in the laundry, kitchen, and on a built-in hutch in the dining area bridged the gap between the separate zones. From there, the room was layered with exquisite design details to convey the overall tone of elegance mixed with casual charm. Perimeter cabinetry painted in French Vanilla enfolds the kitchen in warm, neutral color that plays nicely against the dark wood. Crown molding, elegant trim, and corner columns added to the island fine-tune the room's character. Polished granite countertops sprinkled with flecks of burgundy and brown echo the cherry cabinet color. A detailed ogee edge treatment adds stunning style and creates a focal point on the island.

Elsewhere in the kitchen, oak flooring and hand-bevelled backsplash tile lend rustic texture that creates a muted contrast when juxtaposed against the polished stone.

Above An under-mounted sink with a stainless bowl is set beneath the island top. It improves the function of the kitchen without distracting from the smooth profile of the polished granite surface.

EAST-SIDE CHIC

Merging two apartments into one produced a sumptuous space,
perfectly proportioned for elegant dining or family gatherings.

For one New York couple, a recent marriage meant merging two smaller households into one large-scale home to accommodate their newly formed family. Though the need for more space was obvious, the question was where to find it. Happily, the answer turned out to be just next door. The purchase of an adjacent apartment in the Upper East Side building allowed the couple to design an expansive kitchen and dining area laden with amenities and detailed with interestingly textured materials.

New York City architect Louise Braverman, hired by the couple, sculpted a magnificent kitchen and dining room at the core of the reconfigured space. Her inspired interpretation, best described as 'textural modernism,' artfully layers the contemporary space with pleasing panoply of subtle geometric pattern, diaphanous fabric, and shimmering, reflective surfaces.

Previous page The spacious dining table is designed to accommodate larger dinner parties and family gatherings, while a small booth in the kitchen creates a cozy spot.

Previous page The glassware collection is lit from the inside of the cabinet, creating a bright spot at the end wall.

Top A sliding wall, crafted of stainless steel topped with translucent glass, anchors a transitional cooking and dining space that adapts to the family's needs.

Right A 21st century update of a mid-century dining booth incorporates a glass table, modern lighting, built-in storage, and smart technology.

Left Subway tiles, a stainless steel switch panel, and soft vinyl flooring are key details in this area.

Left Pale reflective surfaces shine in this kitchen design.

Above Subtle lighting makes the space feel entirely different at night.

Right A wall of kitchen units sits to the rear of the living space, with a large rectangular island featuring the sink and preparation area.

Left Pale reflective surfaces shine in this kitchen design.

Above Subtle lighting makes the space feel entirely different at night.

Opposite page A kitchen wall covered in cork creates an oversized bulletin board to display favorite photos, travel mementos, and family announcements.

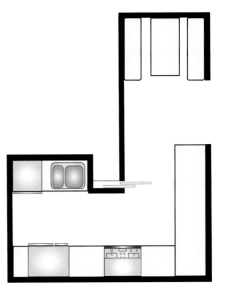

Above Removing walls to merge two apartments into one created a large living space. The flexible kitchen flexible has a casual dining booth.

The apartment's interior kitchen posed the project's primary challenge. According to New York building codes, windowless kitchens are limited in size and must be fully enclosed. While some might view these guidelines as a recipe for a dark, boxy space, Braverman rose to the challenge by designing a beautiful sliding wall that met the city's requirements and filled the cooking zone with coveted natural light.

The wall divides the formal and informal areas of the kitchen and dining room when it is open and completely slides into the wall and out of view when it is closed. Her inspired solution produced the best of all possible worlds; an expansive space for dining with family and a group of friends, along with a more intimate dining room for quiet, candlelit suppers.

The stainless-frame system features patterned fabric set between two panels of translucent glass, creating privacy while still allowing softly diffused light to pass through to the kitchen. A wood beam provides the necessary structural support and houses the mechanism's hardware. Below the glass panels, textured maple base cabinets form a functional half-wall that further delineates the kitchen from the dining area.

The custom cabinets, faced with elegant, layered wood doors, provide generous storage for dinnerware, serving

platters and table linens, and they open on both sides to allow convenient access.

A variation of the custom maple cabinets located in the formal area was chosen for the kitchen. In the cooking and food prep area, flat paneled doors strike a streamlined tone that fits the function of the space. Since this is a kitchen that is used, rather than simply admired, low-maintenance materials were a must. With that in mind, smooth slate countertops in a sophisticated matte finish create durable, stain-resistant work surfaces that introduce an added layer of natural texture to the kitchen.

Iridescent sheet vinyl flooring in an eye-catching circle pattern plays the perfect foil to the clean lines and straight edges found elsewhere in the space. This resilient flooring is soft underfoot, which is especially welcome when a chef has to stand for long periods of time.

Angled against the cooking area, a butler's pantry makes a stylish bar for cocktail parties, or acts as extra counterspace when large meals are prepared.

Upper cabinets, lit from within and framed with textured glass doors, create a luminous display for glassware collections. Across the kitchen is a fresh interpretation of a mid-20th century classic: The built-in dining booth. Braverman's updated design features a chic glass table set on a solitary, stainless-steel spike; a minimalist touch that maximizes legroom. Built-in benches slide open for storage and seat backs, covered in vintage fabric, add cushioned comfort.

Top Recessed fixtures built into the maple support beam add subtle accent lighting for evening dining.

Above Custom maple base cabinets separate the kitchen and dining areas, adding elegant texture as well as convenient storage accessible on both sides.

A wall-mounted television situated next to the booth enables people to catch up on the day's headlines or work online.

The dining space resonates with style; however, family function was at the heart of every design decision made. The generously sized table seats eight and is used everyday. Durable, mahogany toned wood flooring has the reputation of showing little wear even after years of heavy use.

Adjustable recessed lighting illuminates a full range of tasks. While the use of lighting as a decorative feature is downplayed, the exception is a chandelier that makes a shimmering centerpiece over the dining room table. The fixture is made up of a collection of dazzling hand-cut crystals suspended from a simple aluminum bar.

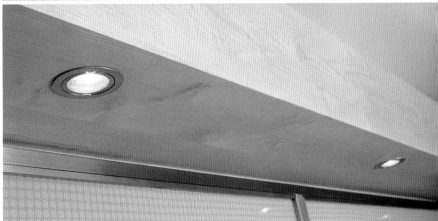

Top The end of a dining room unit was the ideal place for a small wine refrigerator.

Center A detail of the recessed lighting on the dining room side of the partition.

Right To make the most of every inch of space, dining benches were fitted with pull-out drawers.

A carefully-considered remodel restores an elegant Manhattan kitchen to its original splendor.

SMART GALLEY REVIVAL

The phrase "good as new" somehow falls short of describing what Manhattan kitchen designer Paul St. James was able to accomplish in the remodeled kitchen of an apartment on the city's Upper West Side. In fact, when St. James was finished with the space, he rendered it better than new. That is because the designer traveled back in time to uncover the materials, style, and period detail originally found in the early 20th-century building, and brought them into the present with stunning results.

His clients, a young couple with small children, loved the apartment's Pre-War character and appreciated the rich architectural legacy of the building. The kitchen, however, did not quite live up to the family's expectations. Last remodeled in the 1970s, the small galley space lacked warmth and charm and featured flat-paneled laminate cabinets as well as a hodgepodge of aging

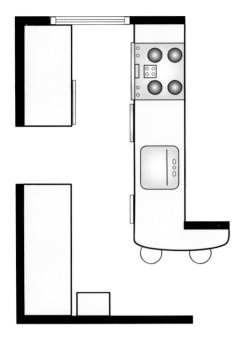

Above Reconfiguring the floor plan to transform a maid's room into a dining room updated the kitchen.

D E S I G N   S U M M A R Y

▶ Linen-White Painted Cabinetry

▶ Raised Panels and Glass Doors

▶ Polished Stone Surfaces

Remodeling and construction are rarely without challenges and limitations, and never more so than when the project is located on the sixth floor of bustling residential building. Of primary concern was a network of gas and plumbing risers that ran up through the building to service the apartments on each floor. Coincidentally, the utility lines were situated in the wall between the kitchen and maid's room. Rather than relocate the lines, a costly and complicated undertaking, the kitchen and dining area was designed around them. Hence, the basic layout of the kitchen remains unchanged.

Now, the rooms are connected by way of a convenient pass-through between upper and lower cabinets as well as a wide passageway that separates the kitchen and the new dining area.

Linen-white cabinets with a glossy, painted finish anchor the signature Park Avenue style of the kitchen. The classic look is characterized by raised panel cabinets, glass doors, and stone countertops.

While the traditional lines and formal feel of basic design echo the past, fresh details and modern day amenities update the space. Polished pewter hardware punctuates doors and drawers, and the dishwasher and refrigerator are outfitted with matching panels to integrate the appliances into surrounding cabinetry.

appliances. In addition, a small maid's room tucked away behind the kitchen represented wasted space that the couple needed to press into service to accommodate their growing family.

St. James came up with a two-fold plan: Step one was to update the floor plan by opening up the space between the kitchen and maid's quarters enabling the maid's room to become a family dining area. Step two involved restoring the kitchen's original grandeur with a palette of materials that paid homage to the building's century-old style.

Previous page and left An elegant mix of classic materials, including granite and wood flooring, restored the kitchen space to its early 19th-century style.

A 30" (75cm) commercial-style gas range, perfectly proportioned to fit the scale of the kitchen, is topped with a space-saving microwave oven. Eliminating a base cabinet made way for a wine refrigerator, a feature St. James frequently incorporates into the kitchens he designs. His rationale: When summer heat forces residents to turn off airconditioning and head for weekend retreats, the small refrigerator preserves the wine regardless of how high the temperature and humidity might climb in the apartment.

Polished granite countertops, finished with a simple edge treatment, make a striking statement in the kitchen. The gray-green Verde Lavearas stone is stain-resistant and less prone to cracking than other varieties of granite, making it an excellent choice for kitchen surfaces. On one side of the room, the stone forms a shallow backsplash and wraps around to form a smart breakfast bar

Top left A base cabinet was replaced with a wine refrigerator.

Center left Subway tiles updated.

Right Storage features use every bit of space.

Far right Raised panels on the dishwasher (and refrigerator) integrate the appliances with surrounding cabinetry.

Right Honey oak flooring adds warmth to the kitchen.

Middle A pull-out cutting board.

Bottom A cutlery drawer is near a food preparation area.

beyond the pass-through. In another nod to the building's heritage, the opposite side of the kitchen features a backsplash of classic subway tile, updated in grey and accented with a pale yellow border. Honey-toned oak flooring, installed in both the kitchen and dining area, adds a warm layer of natural texture that visually connects the two spaces.

Thoughtful attention to period detail is responsible for the kitchen's appealing form; however, well-considered storage plays a strong supporting role in making the space function well for a family. Cabinet interiors fitted with accessories such as cutlery trays, shelves for small appliances, and non-perishable foods exemplifies good use of every bit of space in the kitchen by keeping contents organized and surfaces clear.

Good organization is an important aspect of any well-run kitchen, and that challenge is even greater in galley-size kitchens where space is at a premium and countertop clutter can make the room feel closed in.

While the basic area of the kitchen remained the same before and after the remodeling project, a pass-through window and a connection to the adjoining room creates the illusion of a much larger space. More importantly, reconfiguring the floor plan gave the family much needed space while still preserving the architectural integrity of an historic New York building.

ECLECTIC MIX

A bright and spacious kitchen thoughtfully detailed with neutral tone and textured surfaces creates a brilliant backdrop for a personal collection.

Home-owner Stacy Trachten wears many hats. She is a busy mother of three, has her own interior design business and in her spare time, she loves to browse tag sales, flea markets, and local antique stores in search of charming treasures for her kitchen. A passionate collector, Stacy's outings have yielded a captivating assortment of porcelain plates, teapots and canister sets, all in need of a permanent home.

Above A spacious kitchen with a sit-down casual dining area anchors the central living space of the home.

Stacy's design philosophy is straightforward: Steer clear of trends and bold color on dominant elements to craft a neutral canvas easily adaptable to a variety of design and entertaining scenarios. In her large New England kitchen, she did just that. Using white birch cabinets as the starting point, she skillfully created a monochromatic showcase for her constantly-changing collection of found treasures.

The white cabinetry features raised paneled doors (lightly rubbed with a cocoa stain to show depth and detail) which reach from floor to ceiling around the perimeter of the kitchen. To visually raise the height of the kitchen, upper cabinets were capped with glass framed boxes that fill in the soffit space. Lit from within, the small cabinets make a striking display that bathes the kitchen in a golden glow, particularly at night when lights are low. Matching panels integrate appliances to create a seamless look; the only break in the wall cabinets comes from a sculpted stainless-steel ventilation hood above the kitchen's commercial cooktop.

Above the sink, a large skylight floods the room with natural light, highlighting the room's intricate wood detailing. A wide pass-through into the family room further reinforces the open feel of the space and connects the kitchen to the adjacent social area of the home.

Bullnose-edged, solid- surface countertops, hand-crafted backsplash tile, and white ceramic floor tile complement the cabinetry and round out the kitchen's muted materials palette.

A sumptuous center island surrounded by wide passageways is perfect for large gatherings. Recently, the family hosted 80

┌─────────────────────────────────────┐
│ **DESIGN SUMMARY**   │
│   │
│ ➤ Monochromatic color scheme   │
│ ➤ Solid surface and granite countertops │
│ ➤ Cocoa-stained birch cabinets   │
└─────────────────────────────────────┘

people for a charity fundraising dinner; a feat made possible by the kitchen's generous proportions. On those special occasions, the large island makes a spacious buffet with enough room for guests to comfortably circulate. Topped with granite and accented with furniture style columns, glass-paneled produce bins, and a wine rack, the island forms the kitchen's focal point.

Additionally, convenient electrical outlets on the side of the island expand its role for entertaining by making it possible to use blenders, chafing dishes, and other small appliances in the center of the room.

In a corner of the kitchen, a comfortable dining nook is where more intimate family meals are enjoyed. A painted pine dining set with charming checkerboard detail was discovered on a family trip to Colorado and shipped home. Family-friendly faux-leather, used on the benches, looks surprisingly like the real thing; however, being able to clean this fabric with soap and water makes it a better choice (than real leather) for a home with young children. Pine shelves, backed with beadboard, rise to the ceiling and wrap the dining area in a display of antiques, knick-knacks, and collectibles that define the character of the cozy and welcoming space.

AT THE BEACH

Glistening blue water, spectacular sunsets, and an endless parade of sailboats are the backdrop for this cottage-style kitchen in a home by the sea.

To fully appreciate this remodeled kitchen, you must first consider its spectacular surroundings. The home, situated in a sheltered cove along a quiet stretch of coastline, features water views from every room. Gentle waves break softly on the sandy beach just outside the living room, and from the kitchen window you can see small sailboats leave the shelter of the marina and head out to sea.

It was against this blissful backdrop that homeowner Susan Unger formulated a kitchen design scheme that would complement, rather than complete with, the idyllic setting.

Unger and her husband combed the coast for a year and a half before happening upon the waterfront lot, and the quaint, seventy-year-old home that came with it. The aged structure was sound; however, dark rooms and an antiquated floor plan blocked light and limited access to the home's exquisite, panoramic views.

Top Brushed stainless-steel cabinet hardware introduces a soft, metallic tone to the pristine, all-white kitchen.

Above Blue-and-white plates are placed on display on the marble countertop.

Right The custom cherry wood island top is the entertaining center of the kitchen. Two stools provide casual seating.

Unger's mission was clear from the start: She wanted a bright, beautiful kitchen visually connected to the water, and large enough to welcome family and friends who came for long, leisurely weekends at the beach.

A childhood of summers spent on Nantucket Island sparked the homeowner's love of simple cottage style. She also liked the idea of layering the kitchen with crisp, white surfaces to contrast with the shimmering blue water. Even though Unger knew exactly the look she was going for in

Left This view encompasses the new dry-goods pantry (behind the single door). The spacious, light living room is behind the glass-fronted cabinets.

Above The classically-styled bridge faucet is a vintage reproduction of an elegant fixture from the early 1900s.

Right A built-in shelf unit separates the kitchen and the entrance foyer. A guest bathroom is located opposite this divider.

the kitchen and the rest of the house, photos clipped from home design magazines helped fine-tune the vision. Cutting out the pictures of cabinets, appliances, fixtures and features that appealed to her, she essentially laid the kitchen out on paper. Unger then took her ideas to an architect and a kitchen designer, who helped finalize the plans.

Adding windows in the kitchen space was the priority. To accomplish this, existing upper cabinets were removed from either side of where the sink was located, and the wall was lined with a row of windows that frame the view and flood the kitchen with light. The only space added to the room was a small bump-out behind the sink that cleverly draws the eye to the windows and ultimately to the small boat marina visible from the front of the home.

Eliminating a wall between the kitchen and living room brought in additional light and accessed views of the beach and ocean. Next, one of two doorways that opened into the old living room was closed off and a set of stairs was removed (and placed elsewhere) to make room for a built-in hutch that runs the length of the new wall. Now there is a wide opening to the large living space, which is easily accessed from the entry area adjacent the kitchen. Here, too, is

the guest bathroom, and the pantry for dry goods is set into the wall locatedd opposite the new kitchen.

The cornerstone of the new design is a large, delightfully-detailed center island brimming with storage features. In addition to a built-in wine rack and some shelves for cookbooks, deep drawers contain everyday dinnerware that was relocated from upper cabinets. On one end of the island, graceful furniture-style legs anchor a casual seating where friends can sit and chat to Susan Unger while she prepares the meal.

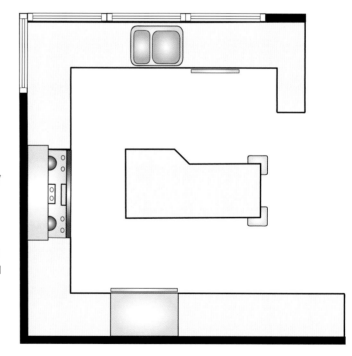

Plan Adding a bank of windows and eliminating a wall between the kitchen and living room made the most of water views and created a more functional floor plan.

On top of the new island is a cherry wood surface that creates a wide work space for serving large meals; the unique wood tone has been created by a water-resistant marine finish that's typically used on boats and bars. Unger first came across the finish several years ago and tucked the idea away, bringing it out for this situation.

Gas utility lines are uncommon along the New England coast, so a large propane tank was installed on the property to fuel the commercial-style range. Elsewhere, a brushed stainless finish on the range hood, dishwasher, and refrigerator coordinates with the hardware to create a neutral design element against the white background.

Below

With space at a premium in the kitchen, recessing the microwave into an upper cabinet next to the refrigerator recovered valuable counterspace.

Top left At night, the glass shelves become a focal point in the kitchen thanks to recessed downlights in the top of the cabinets.

Top right A small drawer next to the range locates frequently used spices and seasonings close to the cooking range.

Above Deep storage drawers in the island are used to store favorite dinnerware.

Painted cabinets and a shiny, ceramic tile backsplash visually enlarge the space and impart an open, expansive feel. Classic Carrera marble countertops on the periphery of the kitchen were inspired by the couple's travels to Italy. While visiting private homes, and peeking in the kitchen, they noted that the marble countertop surface retained its good looks, even after generations of wear. The less-reflective, honed finish is easier to maintain than polished stone, and balances the glossier surfaces. A white farmhouse sink and a reproduction faucet are set into the countertop. These timeless details are among Unger's favorite features. The wide porcelain bowl is generously proportioned to accommodate a variety of tasks, including Unger's most-treasured weekend activity; bathing her one-year-old grandson after an afternoon at the beach.

Above left A small kitchen bar tucked into a tiny corner cabinet is a nice touch that comes in handy for frequent entertaining.

Center A row of pretty windows added above the sink offers a view of the inlet leading to a marina.

STAINLESS
STAR

With the children grown, a Connecticut couple created a dream kitchen that combines a love of cooking with spectacular stainless style.

Good things come to those who wait. Just ask the Milford couple whose recent renovation of a 20-year-old kitchen brought their vision of the perfect space to life. With his background as a builder of high-end custom homes, and her years of experience in the restaurant industry, the couple had the advantage of knowing exactly what they wanted. Together, they styled a stunning, stainless-steel chef's kitchen personalized for the way they cook and entertain.

The size and layout of the old kitchen were fine the way they were, allowing the homeowners to remodel within the existing footprint and avoid the disruption of moving walls or relocating plumbing or electrical lines. This meant they could focus on the style and function of the space.

Here, sleek, stainless-steel cabinets anchor the fresh design of the kitchen and create the room's smooth silhouette. The wife's experience in commercial kitchens led to the decision to choose stainless cabinets. In addition to the clean look, she appreciated the durability and easy care that the surface offers. Flat panel cabinet doors and drawers add elegance along with low maintenance.

Top A single faucet with a brushed stainless-steel finish adds sculptural beauty to the sink area.

Above Warm copper accents and a brushed finish tone down the stainless effect.

For the homeowner, less time spent on cleaning up meant more time to enjoy daily visits with her grandchildren, who live nearby.

Surrounding an entire space with stainless steel might have made the kitchen feel cold and industrial; however, warm accents, natural texture, and a brushed metal finish make the mood warm and welcoming. Copper trim runs along the top and bottom of upper cabinets, creating a subtle band of tone-on-tone contrast that also conceals an under-cabinet light rail.

Sparkling glass backsplash tile winds its way around the kitchen and culminates in a shimmering tiled wall around the sink that extends to the ceiling. The inspiration for the mosaic tile comes from their impressive art glass collection, culled from the couple's extensive travels, and displayed throughout

Left A custom-designed desk with telephone and computer is the kitchen's command center.

Above A built-in gas grill was the only feature preserved from the original kitchen.

Right Brushed stainless steel, with its low maintenance and durability, is an ideal material for kitchen cabinets.

Left Copper and stainless steel trim above the refrigerator integrate the appliances and the surrounding cabinets.

Above Strong European hinges were chosen to handle the weight of the cabinets.

Above right Honey-brown slate floor tiles infuse the kitchen with an earthy texture.

Right A built-in pantry features 10 roll-out drawers that hold an assortment of spices and non-perisherable foods.

the home. Also at the sink, the graceful lines of a sculpted, single lever faucet adds a footnote of modern elegance.

Mahogany-toned granite countertops paired with mottled slate floor tiles work in tandem to create the kitchen's hardworking surfaces and add rich texture that further soften the stainless steel.

In the heart of the room, a six-burner gas cooktop, set into an expansive island,

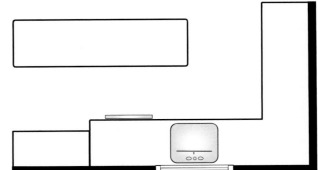

Above The only change to the layout was to replace a peninsular with a central island.

Left The drawer at the end of the island was designed to integrate it to the rest of the unit.

forms the functional center of the space. The kitchen's efficient layout places each of the work zones within a few feet of one another, allowing the cook to easily move from one task to the next without wasted steps. Across from the cooktop is a favorite feature of the kitchen; a built-in gas grill that is used nearly every day. Rounding out the superb selection of high-performance appliances are a commercial dishwasher, built-in refrigerator and large capacity conventional and convection ovens.

When the owners entertain guests, meals are served in the home's formal dining room, adjacent the kitchen; however, a pretty, glass-topped table across from the island is where family and friends frequently gather to chat with their hosts while dinner is prepared.

Next to the sink, a built-in custom stainless-steel desk provides a practical work area and it is here that the owner organizes the household's paperwork. Though there is a full office located on the second floor of the home, incorporating this smaller workstation close to the kitchen creates a more convenient place for her to write notes, store recipes, pay bills, or check emails while she is waiting for the meal to cook.

An open, airy kitchen
is full of charm and
convenience thanks
to a contemporary
floor plan and details
befitting the heritage
of the home.

WHITE ELEGANCE

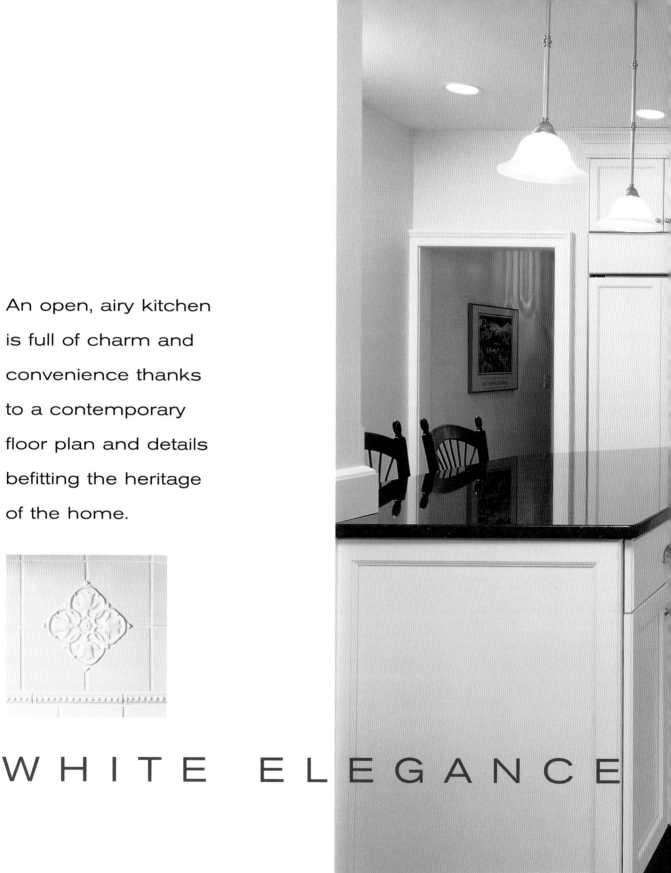

Kitchen design has come a long way in the past eighty years. The case in point is a Connecticut home where the cramped cooking area was little more than a tiny alcove with a range and refrigerator. Barely big enough to turn around in, the space offered little in the way of storage or counterspace, and no dining area.

However, the irresistible charm of the quaint New England home won the hearts of the new buyers who went ahead with the purchase in spite of its drawbacks. To solve the kitchen puzzle, they turned to designer Bettyann Peck for help in devising a plan that would modernize the outdated space, without compromising its connection to the eighty-year-old home.

Peck's clients, a busy family of four that includes two teenage children, are active in the local community. They enjoy preparing meals together and entertain frequently. The family also wanted a wide-open kitchen with workspace for community projects, as well as a welcoming place where the teenagers and their friends could do homework or socialize.

Gaining the necessary space for the project involved eliminating non-load-bearing interior walls and enclosing a small, covered

Above A small television and video player tucked inside an upper cabinet disappears from view when not in use.

Right An existing support column became in architectural feature.

DESIGN SUMMARY

▶ Painted cabinets with a low-sheen finish

▶ White oak flooring

▶ Furniture detailing

▶ Retro lighting, fixtures, and hardware

▶ High-gloss granite countertops

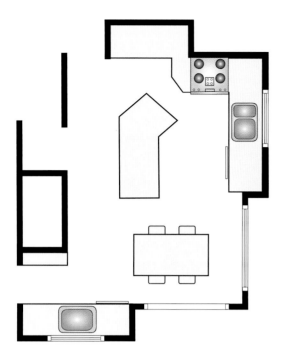

Above Eliminating non load-bearing walls and enclosing a small porch created the kitchen's open and airy floor plan.

porch located just outside kitchen. When an existing support column had to remain, Peck turned it into an architectural feature to anchor one end of the kitchen island. While adding extra space expanded the room's possibilities, raising the ceiling to the roof line defined its character. The new space, larger higher than before, created the airy feel that was the foundation for the rest of the design.

Bigger isn't always better, especially when it comes to kitchen design. Without proper planning, there can be a fine line between "open and airy" and "cold and cavernous." Here, the challenge was met with details inspired by the home's architectural style. These details balance the large room's proportions and convey an intimate atmosphere. Retro-design pendant lights, vintage-style fixtures, appliance panels, and

furniture detailing work together to convey a feeling of gracious charm.

Painted white cabinetry, the room's largest design element, is elegant in its simplicity. Raised paneled doors with delicate trim, plus a combination of staggered height and depth, fluted columns, dentil molding, glass doors, and a corner display shelf provide layers of visual interest.

The kitchen's understated tenor comes from a studied mix of materials. A low-sheen finish on the upper and lower cabinets complements the glossy, onyx colored granite countertops. The same is true of the backsplash, where four styles of white and cream ceramic tile create a rich texture throughout.

A sloping ceiling delineates the dining area, establishing a subtle sense of shelter above the space. Beyond the dining area, the homeowners added a butler's pantry to create a convenient preparation area for catered parties. It can also act as a beverage center for less formal occasions. Fitted with a sink, storage cabinets, and a dishwasher, the pantry serves the kitchen, the formal dining room, and the outside patio.

Wrapped within the kitchen's form is its function. Tall cabinets that rise to the ceiling create drama, along with extra storage. The generously-sized granite island

Right
Extending the island on one side created room for dining; a built-in bookshelf was carved out of a little used corner of the kitchen.

top adds high-gloss glamour. Even the angled cabinet at the end of the island was strategically placed. In addition to visually breaking up the kitchen's long lines, pull-outs inside the unit offer storage for pots and pans close to the cooking zone. The result of such meticulous planning is a functional kitchen that hums with activity, and where every nook and cranny in it serves a specific purpose.

Opposite page
Retro lighting, hardware, and fixtures add period details that convey the kitchen's overall tone of elegance.

Below left   The well-appointed butler's pantry and, **below right**, a detail of the tile pattern.

Bottom
The oak flooring was matched to wood elsewhere in the home.

BEAUX ARTS STYLE

Blending classic architectural form with modern style, a kitchen designer sculpts a luxuriously detailed space to reflect a new way of living.

Kitchen styles may come and go, but according to kitchen designer Mick deGulio, lifestyle shifts have lasting power. In this kitchen, deGulio has created a "living" room that features cooking zones as one of the many function areas of the multi-use space. This is his modern masterpiece: A sleek Beaux Arts-style space that combines a medley of classic materials with contemporary design elements to form an sophisticated multi-use room.

In the kitchen area, cabinetry on the perimeter is the utilitarian anchor of the space. The modular base cabinets are designed to maximize storage space, and the

Left Classic materials create a modern kitchen with timeless appeal.

▶ Carerra marble surfaces

▶ Painted cabinets

▶ Walnut flooring

▶ Pale walls

▶ Metallic accents

full extension drawers in the cooking zone offer easy access to cookware and supplies stored near the range.

Understated glass-fronted upper cabinets are topped with display boxes to increase the amount of accessible storage. This combination strikes a slim profile that presents a 21st-century take on clean-lined Craftsman style.

Classic Carerra marble surfaces impart a timeless elegance that wraps the cooking zone in a layer of cool texture. In addition, the stone's shadowy grey marbling complements the cabinets' crisp, white lacquer finish. Behind the range, retractable marble panels slide open to reveal counter level storage for spices and small appliances.

Elsewhere in the cooking zone, metallic accents in the form of a substantial stainless-steel range hood, an overhead pot rack, and polished nickel cabinet hardware form a neutral design element contrasting with the kitchen's backdrop of white cabinets, stone surfaces, and the rich, wide-plank walnut flooring.

A sleek, minimal island marks the transition between the cooking and social areas of the room. The working side of the island includes an extra-wide stone sink fitted

Opposite page Mirrors installed above the sink in the butler's pantry form a focal point that visually elongates the compact space.

Above Retractable marble panels on both sides of the range slide across to reveal convenient storage space for cooking supplies and small appliances.

Above A marble ledge runs the width of the cooking zone; a display of art sits above the stainless hood under accent lighting.

Above right Repeating polished marble surfaces on countertops and the backsplash gives the kitchen a sleek, sophisticated edge.

Right Furniture-style base cabinets are fitted with deep drawers to maximize storage close to the cooking zone.

with a teak drain board and a stunning, platinum-finish faucet and spray attachment. Electrical outlets in the side of the island are concealed behind flip-down doors when not in use. At the opposite end, the marble extends to create a spacious seating area.

Next to the kitchen, a classically-styled butler's pantry echoes many of the same design elements used in the kitchen to fashion a well-appointed presentation area for catered meals. Mosaic-tile flooring, painted cabinets and a reproduction faucet evoke the vintage style of the 1930s; however, modern features such as flat-panel cabinet doors, a brushed nickel, apron-front sink and contemporary lighting balance the old with the new. Honey-toned maple countertops add lustrous, durable surfaces. A sliding panel, tucked under an upper cabinet, enables serving platters and dinnerware to be passed between the two spaces.

Once the design of the food preparation area was in place, deGulio personalized the less-formal living areas with furnishings and collections that reflect his individual style. Comfortable upholstered chairs, an antique butcher block, and a grand armoire blend with the kitchen's more structured elements to set a gracious tone for both casual dining and relaxation.

Above A detail of the rich walnut flooring.

Right The black and white ceramic floor design runs around the perimeter of the butler's pantry.

A modern kitchen makeover opens up
new possibilities in an apartment that
features sweeping city views.

Opposite
Clean lines and
sleek surfaces set
the modern mood
of the kitchen.

Right
A recessed niche
in a corner of the
kitchen creates a
colorful backdrop
for the owner's art
collection.

Below
A stainless-steel
light bar accents
upper cabinets.

POINT OF VIEW

Interior walls and an outdated floor plan blocked more than natural light from the kitchen of a spacious Central Park West apartment. The design also downplayed one of the apartment's finest features, spectacular three-sided views of the city. Award-winning New York-based architect Louise Braverman, hired to redesign the kitchen, restored the magnificent vistas and layered the space with modern style.

Used as a cultural retreat by a couple who commute to the city each weekend from their suburban home, the apartment serves as the frequent gathering spot for their large extended family. Braverman first enlarged the kitchen by borrowing space from the adjacent dining room and then transformed it with an inspired interplay of clean lines, repeated pattern, and translucent texture. The result is a layered architectural statement that is simple, without feeling sparse.

Replacing an interior wall between the dining room and kitchen with patterned glass-paneled pocket doors brings light into the kitchen without sacrificing privacy in the dining room. With the doors open, the spectacular city views from the next room are visible from the kitchen. When they are closed; the dining room reverts back to a separate space for intimate dining, or an impromptu guest room for the couple's grandchildren.

Braverman's space shifting approach to the design of the apartment skillfully creates rooms that respond to the constantly changing needs of the active family. The pocket doors also illustrate the architect's concept of layering the interior with

Left A mundane task gets a chic makeover in a laundry alcove tucked into a passageway of the kitchen.

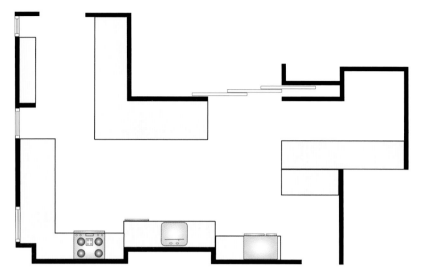
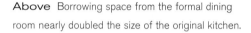

Opposite The kitchen's built in dining table is poised to take advantage of the spectacular city views that can be seen from the dining room.

Below Stunning stone surfaces offer more than meets the eye. In addition to textural beauty, they represent durability in the busy kitchen.

Above Borrowing space from the formal dining room nearly doubled the size of the original kitchen.

architectural transitions that offer a unique, sequential view at every turn as one moves through the apartment toward the views of the cityscape. The effect might be compared to light passing through a prism. Turned one way, you regard the space in a certain light, slightly tilt the crystal and you gain an entirely different, yet equally fascinating, perspective.

To connect the modern kitchen with traditional architectural features found elsewhere in the apartment, European cherry wood cabinets were matched to the dining room's original parquet floors.

Minimally-detailed flat paneled doors rise to the ceiling, and help establish the kitchen's clean-lined countenance. Set against the wood, a run of stainless-steel cabinets and appliances, topped with a glazed tile backsplash, creates contrast and delineates the kitchen's cooking zone.

Smoke-grey Pietro Cardoza stone, selected for both the countertop and the floor, adds elegance, as well as durability; the stone surface is also easy to maintain.

Where a more traditionally-styled kitchen might rely upon molding and trim to provide architectural detail, Braverman uses variation of form. In this case, a series of inverted L-shapes that echo the kitchen layout were integrated into the ceiling to create yet another layer of interest that heightens kitchen's visual appeal.

Stainless-steel light bars above the walnut cabinets beautifully highlight this feature by directing light up to illuminate the soffit, and casting the workspace in a soft, appealing glow. The L form appears again on a stationary table anchored between the kitchen and dining room. Like the rest of the kitchen, the highly-styled modern island is

designed to be flexible. It can serve as a workspace or a casual dining area when the glass pocket doors are closed, or it can be a staging area for meals served in the dining room when the doors are open for business.

At the bottom of the L-shape layout, a laundry alcove makes the most of a little-used passageway between the central space of the kitchen and a half-bath at the opposite end. Situating the super-quiet washer and dryer in a far corner of the apartment adds convenience without the noise.

To accommodate plumbing lines, the appliances were placed on an elevated platform. Raising them off of the floor enabled easy access to the washer and dryer, without the need for anyone to bend down low.

As a finishing touch, original artwork and an elegant sideboard round out the laundry-chic look in this area.

WORKING WITH DESIGN PROFESSIONALS

Regardless of the scope of a project or the size of a budget, every homeowner will benefit from a consultation with a design professional. The reason is that few of us are trained to take a three-dimensional approach to the design of our surroundings.

We might know what we want, and what we like, but be less equipped to know the best way to turn that dream into reality. Even more importantly, design professionals are trained to see the potential of a project.

The challenge is to find a design expert that best suits the scale of your project. If your new kitchen involves major structural changes, a relocation of utilities, or an addition to your home, consider an architect with residential experience. If you plan to remodel within the existing footprint of your current kitchen without significant structural changes, hire a certified kitchen designer. In some cases, it may make sense to consult both types of experts; the architect on style, structural issues, and local codes; and the kitchen designer for expertise on cabinetry, appliances, materials, and storage.

Begin the search by asking friends and homeowners in your area for their recommendations. You can also obtain the names of qualified individuals from national organizations that license and certify design professionals, such as The American Institute of Architects (www.aia.org) or The National Kitchen and Bath Association (www.nkba.com).

Interview several professionals before making a final decision. Look at work which reflects your home's architecture, or is simlar to the style of kitchen you want to build.

During the initial consultation, show the professional sketches and photographs that convey your taste, style preference, and design ideas. Also, present a preliminary budget to help guide you toward viable options. At this stage, be prepared to discuss design fees. Is the person willing to negotiate a flat fee for the project, or do they charge an hourly rate? If they bill by the hour, check how much time they expect the project to take. Although design fees vary, estimate the professional's costs to be between five and 15 percent of the project's budget.

Do not hesitate to ask questions or to clarify information. Ask the person to walk you through the project from start to finish in order to understand the process. Review drawings and photographs of their previous projects and ask for references. Also ask if you can visit a completed project to evaluate their work before making a decision.

When you have done your homework, it is important to hear what the architect or kitchen designer has to say about your project. Listen to ideas with an open mind and do not be surprised if your vision of the kitchen evolves as you gather information. Professionals approach design from a different perspective than a homeowner; they may point out possibilities you had not considered, or based upon their experience, they may eliminate options. Always keep in mind that the objective is for the design professional to be guided by your vision and your goals, not the other way around. It is your home, your budget and you are always in control of the project. If the person is not responding to your ideas, or is trying to impose their signature style on you, take that as a cue to move on to the next candidate; communication and a solid working relationship are crucial for success.

Once you have made a decision to hire, set a firm budget, and agreed terms, your project will proceed to the design phase. The architect or kitchen designer will show you an initial set of plans for review and revision. If you require alterations, now is the time to make them. Even small changes to a final design can be costly and cause delays.

MANAGING THE CONSTRUCTION

While meticulous planning will minimize any problems arising during construction projects, they will not be eliminated entirely. From sorting out small issues, such as cleaning up the site daily, to dealing with more pressing matters, such as extended delays or quality of workmanship, the construction process is layered with details and complexities.

Most state governments have a list of organizations that govern contractors, issue licenses, and set specific standards of performance. To understand your rights as a consumer, contact the appropriate organization to familiarize yourself with the regulations before hiring a professional to work on your home. Then put a plan of work in place.

Other points to consider include:

► Draw up contract for signature that states the scope of the project, the estimated cost, a payment schedule, and a reasonable time frame for completion. Include details such as how the contractor plans to seal off the work zone, what time workers will arrive each morning, and that they will clean up the site daily.

► Read the fine print. Many standard contracts outline terms for settling disputes; some limit the homeowners' ability to take legal action. Make all of the changes before signing the agreement.

► Set up a portable file to organize project paperwork and include sections for payments, receipts, and notes of meetings or conversations with the contractor.

► Make a list of questions and/or concerns that arise as the construction progresses. Arrange a weekly meeting with the contractor to review the timetable and resolve issues.

► When construction is complete, conduct a walk-through to inspect cabinets, surfaces, appliances, lighting, outlets, and plumbing before signing off on the project.

► Compile a list of items that need to be addressed and withhold final payment until each matter has been resolved to your complete satisfaction.

INDEX

COMPANIES WHOSE WORK APPEARS IN THIS BOOK

Bilotta Home Center, Inc.,
564 Mamaroneck Avenue,
Mamaroneck, NY 10453,
USA.
www.bilotta.com

Bilotta Kitchens of NY,
Architects' and Designers'
Building,
150 E. 58th St,
NY 10155, USA.
www.bilotta.com

Bilotta Kitchens of Mt
Kisco,
175 Main St, Mt Kisco,
NY 10549, USA.
www.bilotta.com

Wood-Mode Fine Custom
Cabinetry
www.wood-mode.com

Signature Custom
Cabinetry,
434 Springville Rd,
Ephrata, PA 17522.
www.signaturecab.com

Clive Christian of
Greenwich,
40 East Putnam Ave,
Greenwich, CT 06830,
USA.
www.bilotta.com

Bettyann Peck,
Design Consultants, Suite 3F,
17 Hillside St,
Norwalk, CT 06854, USA.
www.designthebest@
aol.com

Viking Kitchen Cabinets,
33-39 John St,
New Britain, CT 06051,
USA.
www.vikingkitchens.com

Paul St James,
St James Kitchens and
Baths,
102 East 19th St,
NY 10003, USA.
www.stjameskitchens.com

Linda Jennings, Jennings
and Company,
436 Woodland Drive
Sarasota, Florida 34234,
USA.
www.jenningsandcompany
.com

Lamperti Associates,
124 Andersen Drive,
San Rafael,
California 94901, USA.
www.lampertiassociates.com

KraftMaid Cabinetry,
15535 South State Ave,
Middlefield, Ohio 44062,
USA.
www.kraftmaid.com

SieMatic Corporation
www.siematic.com

NY Loft,
Distributors of Maistri
Italian Cabinetry,
6 West 20th St,
New York, NY 10011,
USA.
www.nyloft.com

Mark Wilkinson Furniture,
Overton House,
High St, Bromham,
Nr Chippenham,
Wiltshire SN15 2HA,
United Kingdom.
www.mwf.com

Wilsonart Solid Surface,
2400 Wilson Place,
P.O.Box 6110, Temple,
Tx 76503-6610, USA.
www.wilsonart.com